BBC Proms 2021

The BBC presents the 127th season
of Henry Wood Promenade Concerts,
broadcasting every Prom live on
BBC Radio 3

At a Glance

For Season Overview, see pages 91–111 • For Contents, including details of feature articles, see pages 4–5

A Symphonic Trinity

Mozart's last three symphonies, memorably described as 'an appeal to eternity', reflect the summit of his inspiration and ingenuity. The Scottish Chamber Orchestra performs them in trio under its young Russian Principal Conductor, Maxim Emelyanychev.

1 AUGUST

Body Music

Augusta Read Thomas's *Dance Foldings* is inspired by the 'biological ballet' of proteins forming in the human body. It launches a series of Proms commissions reflecting the Royal Albert Hall's aim of celebrating the arts and sciences, in its 150th-anniversary year.

8 AUGUST

Opera Tonic

British soprano Sally Matthews – 'a bright-voiced, touching heroine' (*Opera* magazine) – is among the vocal stars exploring the themes of love, loss and reconnection in an evening offering operatic balm in these current times of uncertainty and separation.

16 AUGUST

MAXIM EMELYANYCHEV

AUGUSTA READ THOMAS

SALLY MATTHEWS

Adama Jalloh (Garcia), Guido Schiefer/Alamy (Piazzolla), Sim Canetty-Clarke (Gardiner)

Jazz Warrior

Born in London to a Guyanese mother and British Trinidadian father, Nubya Garcia has emerged as one of the brightest voices of the British jazz scene. Following her live-streamed set at Glastonbury last year, the saxophonist, composer, bandleader and DJ makes her Proms debut.

18 AUGUST

NUBYA GARCIA

The Tango King

The Proms marks the 100th anniversary of *nuevo tango* creator Astor Piazzolla with a Prom drawing together Antonio Vivaldi's evergreen *The Four Seasons* with the tango king's *The Four Seasons of Buenos Aires*, featuring the perennially youthful violinist and director Joshua Bell.

25 AUGUST *(see also 23 August)*

ASTOR PIAZZOLLA

The Constant Gardiner

One of the great reformers of how early music is heard by modern ears, Sir John Eliot Gardiner conducts his 60th Prom. The programme of Bach and Handel features the English Baroque Soloists, joined by the Monteverdi Choir, which Gardiner founded almost 60 years ago.

1 SEPTEMBER

SIR JOHN ELIOT GARDINER

Contents

6
Welcome
BBC Proms Director David Pickard and BBC Radio 3 Controller Alan Davey introduce the themes and highlights of the 2021 Proms season

8
A Song for Giles
A new short story by novelist Chibundu Onuzo. When Marian joins a gospel choir, she finds it changes her life in unexpected ways

14
Before I Go on Stage
Author and journalist Jessica Duchen delves into the superstitions and rituals of performing musicians past and present

26
Musician, Muse, Motivator
200 years after Pauline Viardot's birth, Natasha Loges outlines the influence the singer and composer had on 19th-century music

30
Secrets in the Void
Following a year of empty concert halls, author and broadcaster Will Self discusses the enigmatic relationship between sound and silence

36
A Gift to the Nation
Lucy Worsley charts the history of the Royal Albert Hall of Arts and Sciences, 150 years after it was opened by Queen Victoria

42
Plunder Enlightening
Describing how composers have stolen and borrowed for centuries, Tom Service asks whether classical music can ever be truly 'original'

52
An Indomitable Maverick
100 years after Ruth Gipps's birth, Jill Halstead examines the impressive legacy of this pioneering and tenacious composer

56
Past Progressive
Author and musicologist Stephen Walsh investigates Stravinsky's creative kleptomania, 50 years after the composer's death

62
A Family Affair
Rebecca Franks previews the Kanneh-Mason siblings' all-star performance of Saint-Saëns's *The Carnival of the Animals* with Michael Morpurgo

66
Tomorrow's Voices
BBC Young Composer judge Kate Whitley catches up with three of the contestants from the 2020 competition

70
Six Degrees of Separation
Aleks Krotoski explores the novel ways in which musicians have sought to connect with audiences during the pandemic

74
Adapt to Survive
As the music industry acclimatises to a socially distant era, Ariane Todes reveals the impact that coronavirus regulations have had on orchestras

78
Ahead of the Curve
Ammar Kalia introduces genre-defying singer-songwriter Moses Sumney ahead of his collaboration with Jules Buckley and the BBC SO

82
Renaissance Resplendence
Caroline Gill celebrates Josquin des Prez, master of the Franco-Flemish polyphonic style, 500 years after his death

84
There once was a ship that put to sea …
Horatio Clare finds new meaning in a generations-old singing tradition

87
The Proms on Radio, TV and Online
Find out how you can follow the Proms this season

91
Season Overview
Current details of all the concerts in the 2021 season

Booking 113
Index of Artists 116
Index of Works 118

Welcome to the 2021 BBC Proms

It feels good to be writing the introduction to the Proms Guide again! Following a very different season last year, in which we responded to the many challenges of the coronavirus pandemic, we are hopeful that this year will mark the start of a journey back to the BBC Proms as we know and love them.

The unique alchemy of the interaction between the artists onstage and the audience in the hall is a huge part of the Proms's allure. Last year, our performers created magic in an empty venue, but this year we look forward to the return of our much-missed audiences, who I am sure will respond with particular enthusiasm after an absence of two years.

Writing this at the end of April, it is unclear how many seats we will be able to offer or whether Promming will be possible but, in the best traditions of the festival, we will ensure that the finest music remains accessible to as many people as possible, with low-priced tickets available for all concerts. For all these booking details, as well as updates on the programming listed in this Guide, you can rely on the Proms website to give you the most up-to-date information.

Creating our six-week season at the Royal Albert Hall and Cadogan Hall amid continuing uncertainty, we have had to balance ambition with caution, old traditions with new realities and firm plans with flexibility. We wanted to

create a 2021 festival with British artists and ensembles at its heart – it feels appropriate, at a time when musicians are rebuilding their careers after over a year of disruption. This is a wonderful opportunity to celebrate the exceptional talent and wide range of the UK's musical community.

2021 marks the Royal Albert Hall's 150th anniversary. The Royal Albert Hall of Arts and Sciences (to give it its full name) has been home to the Proms for the past 80 years and we look to the future with new commissions reflecting both the 'arts' and 'sciences' of that title. This anniversary also gives us an opportunity to showcase the Hall's magnificent Henry Willis organ – played during its opening season in 1871 by no lesser figures than Bruckner and Saint-Saëns.

The organ represents just one aspect of the building's remarkable musical history, having provided the setting for performances by some of the world's most distinguished international artists, working across all musical genres. We continue to marvel at the versatility of a venue that can happily contain such a vast range of music, from the epic to the intimate.

The other major anniversary of 2021 is that of Igor Stravinsky, who died 50 years ago. His music and influence continue to be felt today, just as in his lifetime. His 'borrowing' from other composers has prompted us to explore the ways in which others have looked to the past to shape the future – including

a contemporary response to Josquin des Prez (who died 500 years ago) by Shiva Feshareki, creating a new sound-world from older music.

This Proms season also offers a chance to hear some concert-hall rarities, and a number of composer anniversaries this year provide a cue to put some in the spotlight, including the prolific Malcolm Arnold, as colourful in his film scores as in his symphonies; his much less well-known contemporary Ruth Gipps, whose Second Symphony receives its Proms premiere; the master of the tango, Astor Piazzolla; and Pauline Viardot, one of the most influential figures in 19th-century French music.

During these troubling times, music has played a vital role. Its power to reflect and express so many shades of emotion has helped many of us through long periods of loneliness and isolation. I hope that the 2021 BBC Proms will offer the boost that we all need at the moment, as well as celebrating the splendour of live music and the return of audiences to our concert halls.

As ever, you will find a number of articles in this Guide that explore some of these themes and anniversaries in more detail, with contributions from such distinguished writers as Chibundu Onuzo, Will Self, Tom Service and Lucy Worsley.

David Pickard Director, BBC Proms

Welcome to the 2021 BBC Proms. What a joy it is to write those words in a year when we have, more than ever, turned to music for intellectual and spiritual enrichment, as well as for understanding and insight. At Radio 3, we have worked with musicians to get their music heard in new ways, and against the odds. We too have found new ways – with presenters broadcasting amid sound-deadening duvets and from sheds across the land.

But we have all missed sharing in performances by musicians playing and sitting together. This year's Proms is a celebration of that magical bond between musicians and audience – the rapt silence in which music is willed into being and absorbed – and of music speaking to us anew.

Radio 3 will, as always, be broadcasting every note in superb sound, making the atmosphere palpable to listeners around the world. All of this will be available for 30 days after the end of the season on BBC Sounds, not to mention all 20 TV broadcasts on iPlayer.

So welcome to six weeks of magical music, communion and transcendence at the BBC Proms!

Alan Davey Controller, BBC Radio 3

A Song for Giles

A short story by CHIBUNDU ONUZO
Illustrations by Haley Tippmann

The last time Marian sang in a choir, she was 11. She was tall for her age and stood head and shoulders above Tommy Atkins, the shortest boy in her year. They sang facing the choirmaster, Mr Jones, a balding, tweed-wearing man who stuttered over hard consonants and stumbled over pleasantries. Without music he was a humble creature but the opening chords of Handel's *Messiah* could always transform him into a dragon.

Theirs was a modest choir in a minor North London prep school but Mr Jones took things very seriously. They mimicked him after rehearsals, closing their eyes and swaying in mock ecstasy, flapping their arms like great, flightless turkeys. But for an hour every Friday afternoon they were spellbound by his baton, a slim white wand that controlled their every movement, that bade them rise and sit, made them thunder *fortissimo* or sing as softly as a sigh.

When Marian was 12, she stopped singing in public. Along with puberty came a crushing awareness of her body, her gangly limbs, her acne-sprouting skin, her knees, her elbows, the back of her neck which blushed furiously with little provocation. How had she, in the name of singing, ever dared to open her mouth wide to the world, to bare her gullet like a chick screeching for a worm?

And so Marian became one of those people who sang in the shower, whose voice was only heard mingled with the sound of water striking cast iron, a melody mixed with rain.

In February 2019 Marian's son Giles died in a skiing accident. Her husband Hugh went to France to retrieve the body. Giles was a corpse now, a thing that could be flown in the hold of a plane, next to the suitcases. Marian did not go. They had other children. The other children still needed regular feeding and freshly laundered clothes. Her mother came to help, and her sister, but they could not stay for ever. 'I should be wearing sackcloth and ashes,' Marian thought as she chopped garlic or folded shirts into envelopes.

Giles had been her first child. Once, it was just the two of them. Hugh was a loving but mostly absent father. He had disappeared to work in the mornings, leaving Marian to figure out how to change Giles's nappies, how to burp him, how to rock him to sleep. She took Giles everywhere, strapped to her chest, pushed in the pram, squashed in the public toilet cubicle when she timed things wrong and found herself far from home and needing to pee. Giles had made her a mother and now he was gone: died on his gap year … accidents happen … nobody's fault.

Afterwards, when the funeral was over and Giles was in the ground, when the seasons had changed and grass had grown over his grave, Marian was still not back to 'normal' – Hugh's word, not hers. What was normal? She woke up and drove her other children to school. She spoke to Hugh about his day; she even slept with him but there seemed to be a thin sheet of glass separating her from the rest of the world. To live with her was to bump up against that cold, flat, reflective surface.

Hugh suggested therapy, a grief specialist who, according to her website, had years of experience 'dealing with loss, separation anxiety and unmet expectations'. Hugh did not need therapy. He played squash.

The therapist's office was on the ground floor of a residential building. It was too warm. Marian walked in and began unbuttoning her coat.

'Susan,' the therapist said, standing up from behind her table and offering a hand. She was fatter than her website photograph.

'Marian,' she said, with one arm still in a coat sleeve. In the bin beside Susan's desk were the discarded shiny foils of chocolate wrappers. Susan sat in a straight-backed office chair but there was a couch for Marian.

'You can sit down, lie down, however you're comfortable.'

Marian did not like to lounge in front of a stranger. She sat stiffly, staring straight at Susan.

'How are you today?'

'Same as every day,' Marian said.

'Which is …?'

'I don't know.'

As the sessions rolled past, Marian realised she said those words often to Susan. They didn't talk about Giles. The one time they tried, Marian began to cry and make a low, keening sound. They talked instead about the weather, about how she met her husband, about music.

'Music comes up a lot in our conversations. Do you play an instrument or sing?' Susan asked.

'I once sang in a choir.'

'Why don't you sing any more?'

'I don't know,' Marian said.

Two days after Susan made her music observation, Marian passed the cork noticeboard in her local supermarket and saw a flier advertising 'Hackney Global Community Choir Auditions'. Stylised music notes danced across the bold pink paper.

The auditions were held in the basement of a church in a part of Hackney that was unfamiliar to Marian. She parked in front of a chicken shop with seating for only two people. The red plastic chairs were empty but the shop was full.

In the basement, there were about 10 other people in the waiting area. She wrote her name on the sign-up sheet and sat down next to a girl with purple braids that dangled to her waist. Her nails were long and acrylic, curving forwards like claws, painted alternately in blue and yellow. There was only one other white person in the room, a boy wearing a hoodie with gelled-back hair. Marian wondered if she should have Googled the Hackney Global Community Choir first. One by one their names were read out until it was Marian's turn.

She shrank a little when she walked into the room and saw a panel of judges staring at her: two women and one man.

'Hello, Marian. I'm Gladys,' the woman in the middle said. She spoke in a deep alto, almost a tenor. Her hair was in silver dreadlocks and she raised her chin when she spoke, challenging, daring.

'Hello,' Marian said, her voice sounding thin in her ears.

'What will you be singing for us today?'

'Amazing Grace.' It was the bread and butter of choirs, a safe choice.

'When you're ready.'

She had practised in the shower, going over her breathing and phrasing, but singing in a bathroom was different to singing in front of three strangers. She rushed through the song.

'Thank you,' Gladys said when she was done. 'Can you tell us the name of someone you love?' she asked.

'Giles,' Marian answered without thinking.

'I'm going to ask you to sing that again, but as if you were singing to Giles.'

She got a text a week later, after she'd long given up hope that she would be called back.

'I got in,' she said to Hugh.

'Into what?'

'A choir.'

'I didn't know you'd auditioned for one. Since when do you sing?'

'I sing all the time in the shower,' Marian said.

'I know. I hear you.'

He tried to put an arm around her and she shrugged him away. He was dependable, her husband. It was part of why she had married him. If they'd agreed to meet at 4pm, he would be there waiting at 3.55pm. But sometimes he didn't seem to think about anything but accounting and squash.

'You have a beautiful shower voice. I just didn't know you wanted to sing outside the bathroom.'

'Well, I do.' She slid her hand into his and he gripped her fingers tightly.

Marian arrived 15 minutes early for her first rehearsal with the Hackney Global Community Choir and the room was empty. She waited, until the other members began to trickle in. They nodded in greeting but no-one spoke to her. She stood quietly in the middle of the growing chatter. She caught snippets of conversation.

'I told him, don't chat shit about my mum.'

'Man like Darius. What's good?'

'Yaaasssss, queen. These braids are popping.'

'You alright?' It was the girl she had sat next to at the auditions. Marian recognised the purple braids but the nails were different, green leopard print this time.

'I'm fine, thank you,' Marian said.

'You were at the same audition as me. I'm Temi but most people call me Tems.'

'Marian.'

'How was your audition? Gladys put me through them vocal drills.'

'I just sang one song.'

'Really? Which one?'

'Amazing Grace,' Marian said.

'Me too.'

When Gladys walked into the room, the chatter died down. She wore a loose blue dress that flowed down to her feet and eddied with each step, like waves lapping at her ankles.

'Good evening. I hope you all enjoyed the summer off and are in fine singing voice. Let's welcome Marian and Tems into our soprano section.'

Everyone turned to face them and Marian blushed. It was the first she was hearing that she would be a soprano. As a child, her voice had been clear and piercing but she thought she had lost her range. She stood next to Tems in the front row.

'We'll start with some vocal warm-ups.'

There was a man at the piano, one of the judges from the audition. Like Gladys, he dressed with flair: black suit, silk pocket square, a gleaming bald head as polished as his shoes. He played a chord and Gladys demonstrated the scale she would like them to sing.

Marian sang quietly, almost under her breath. She could hear Tems's voice, loud and strong. 'I am not good enough for this choir,' Marian thought, but she carried on.

She felt at once exposed and protected, singing in public but from the safety of a crowd.

Their voices climbed higher and higher, like birds trying to touch the roof of the sky. First the basses dropped away, then the tenors, then the altos. When Marian stopped singing, most of the sopranos still forged ahead. Five sopranos left, then three, then two, then Tems, breaking out of the atmosphere and soaring into outer space. When her voice finally gave way, the choir erupted into applause and cheering.

'I didn't know I could do that,' Tems whispered to Marian.

> 66 'We're going right back to the roots of gospel music,' Gladys said after Anderson's last note had rung out. 'Going right back to the slaves who made this music to comfort them, to uplift their spirits and bring joy to their hard lives.' 99

They would learn Deep River that first rehearsal. They listened to the classic recording by Marian Anderson, a rich, quivering alto, with hope and sorrow in every tremor of her voice.

'We're going right back to the roots of gospel music,' Gladys said after Anderson's last note had rung out. 'Going right back to the slaves who made this music to comfort them, to uplift their spirits and bring joy to their hard lives.'

Gladys used her hands when she spoke. She projected like an actor on a stage but there was nothing false about her. They were rapt.

They learnt without sheet music, a first for Marian. The melody was not bound to a page but stored in Gladys's mind. She went line by line, in a sort of call and response. She sang and then the sopranos sang back, followed by the altos, then the tenors and basses. It was too much to learn, too much music, a knot of discordant singing, Marian thought.

Things fell together in the last five minutes. Gladys called for a run-through. Some groaned. It was too soon, Marian thought. They were not ready, but Gladys insisted and they began. It was rough in parts, unsure in others, but Marian could see the shape of the harmonies, the rise and swells, the longing of the slaves for the sweet release of death.

When she got home, Hugh was preparing dinner.

'How was it?' he asked.

'I don't know,' Marian almost said, but she stopped herself.

'It was wonderful.'

And then she went upstairs to lie down with her namesake Marian Anderson's voice still ringing in her ears.

In her next therapy session, Marian told Susan about the choir rehearsal.

'I was the only white person my age there.'

'How did you feel about that?' Susan asked.

'I don't know,' Marian said. 'Actually, I do know. I felt guilty that I'd never seen any of them before, even though they all live locally. I mean, Hackney is not a village but still you would think I would have bumped into them somewhere.'

'Where?' Susan asked.

Marian looked up at her therapist. The question was as toneless as all Susan's other questions, but she felt mocked. On her drive home, she studied her neighbourhood. Her family were incomers – 'colonisers' or 'gentrifiers', if you read *The Guardian*. There was a whole tribe of them who came for the Victorian houses with their high ceilings and original features, who crossed postcodes for the bargain buildings that would be twice the price in Hampstead or Richmond. Hugh said they also brought something to the neighbourhood. 'What?' Marian wondered, as she parked in front of her house.

At the next rehearsal, they went over *Deep River* again and began Psalm 23.

'This time we're going to Africa,' Gladys explained. 'I first heard this song on Radio 3. Composed by a Nigerian Bishop, the Right Reverend Ken Okeke. Choral music but with a Nigerian twist.' Gladys sang the opening lines: 'The Lord is my shepherd, I shall not want.'

'How come it's in English?' someone asked.

'Because from the 17th century onwards, the English refused to stay at home.'

Afterwards, Tems said to Marian, 'It was my birthday at the weekend. A few of us are going Nando's, just up the road. You want to come?'

'Yes, please,' Marian said. She was touched to be invited.

They walked, with Tems leading the way and Marian at the rear. She found herself next to a young man who dwarfed her. He was broad and he wore his hoodie pulled up against the cold.

'Brian,' he said. His voice was deep and gentle.

'Marian.'

'You're new, right? How you finding it?'

'Fun but challenging, I think. I've never had to remember so much music in my life.'

'Yeah, I was the same three years ago when I joined. You get used to it. The human memory is powerful.' He put emphasis on the last word, 'pow-aah-full'. It gave rhythm, cadence, revelation to that simple statement. The human memory *was* powerful. She could still remember the feel of Giles's baby head under her chin, his face pressed into her neck, his spit mingling with her skin.

At the restaurant they stood at the entrance until a waitress in a black T-shirt and jeans approached.

'Good evening. How many are we today?'

'Eight,' Tems said.

'Is this your first time here?'

'Yes,' Marian said, when everyone else said, 'No.'

Brian turned to her in amazement. 'You've never been here before? You're in for a treat, boy!'

'All right,' the hostess said, with eight menus in her hand. 'Follow me.'

At the table, they explained how things worked. Order at the counter, wait for your food at the table. It was a mixture of canteen and restaurant.

'How spicy do you like your chicken?' Tems asked. There was a cartoon chilli on the menu, drawn with different bands of colour to indicate different levels of spiciness.

'Lemon and Herb sounds nice,' Marian said.

Brian groaned. 'Lemon and Herb? That's some white-people chicken.'

Everybody froze and turned to Marian. She felt a blush rising, but she slowed her breathing and clasped her hands, a technique she had learnt in therapy.

'Shut up, Brian,' Tems said, breaking the silence.

'It's fine,' Marian said. 'What do you suggest?' she asked him.

'Sorry, I didn't mean nothing by it. Just think, for your first time at Nando's, you should at least, *at least*, go Medium.'

'All right. Medium, then,' Marian said, and the table cheered.

When Marian's food arrived and she bit into the hot chicken, seasoned with a kick of peri-peri spice, Marian wondered why she had never tried it before.

When she got home, her younger daughter Ella was in the living room watching television.

'Hi, Mum,' she said.

Ella had grown in the past few months and she'd changed her hair, cut it short to her shoulders. Hugh must have taken her.

'Hi, Ella,' Marian said, sitting beside her daughter. She was still in her uniform, her blouse hanging out of her tartan skirt.

'Have you ever been to Nando's?' Marian asked.

> 66 It was rough in parts, unsure in others, but Marian could see the shape of the harmonies, the rise and swells, the longing of the slaves for the sweet release of death. 99

'Of course. We used to go all the time.'

'We?'

Her daughter hesitated. 'Me and Giles,' she said.

'It's all right. We can say his name. Giles,' Marian said. She remembered the first time she realised that she could call him but he would never answer.

'Giles,' she said again. The realisation hurt a little less this time.

Rehearsals came and went. With each week Marian grew more confident and sang louder.

'Next week is an open rehearsal,' Gladys announced one evening. 'You can invite your friends and family.'

Hugh came with Ella and Tom, their second son. She saw them when they arrived, sitting up straight on the benches, unzipping but not taking off their coats. The hall took some time to warm up. She waved and they waved back.

As usual, the choir began with their vocal warm-ups. Sam, that was the pianist's name, played the first chord and they sang a scale. Semitone by semitone they climbed until, gradually, the singers began to drop out. Then one or two sopranos began to flag, but Marian kept going. I'll just do one more scale, she thought. One more. Until there were four sopranos, then three, then Marian and Tems – Tems the weekly champion who was smiling her surprise at this new contender. 'One more scale,' Marian thought, 'just one more.' Until she was the only person singing and her voice was ringing clear as a bell peal, surging through the space. When her voice gave out in a gasp, the room erupted in applause.

Gladys, who was standing in front of her, and had drawn near to watch the singing battle, said softly, under the thunder of clapping hands, so only Marian could hear:

'That was for Giles.' ●

Chibundu Onuzo is the author of *The Spider King's Daughter*, *Welcome to Lagos* and *Sankofa*, forthcoming in June. She has a PhD in History from King's College, London.

Haley Tippmann is an American illustrator living in Koblenz, Germany. Her illustrations have been published in FT Magazine, Flow Magazine and The New Yorker.

Before I Go on Stage

JESSICA DUCHEN reveals the preparations and rituals — from the practical to the downright superstitious — that help musicians feel they're ready to face the audience

If you visit the museum at Troldhaugen, Edvard Grieg's former home in Bergen, you might spot several strange figurines in his wife's bureau. One is a toy troll; another a pig with a four-leaved clover in its snout; and, last but not least, a statuette of a frog. The great Norwegian composer, so the story goes, used to bid the troll goodnight; the pig travelled with him as his mascot; and before he went on stage he always stroked the frog on the back for luck.

If it's good enough for Grieg, then it's good enough for us, and the tales of musicians' pre-concert rituals remain an endless source of fascination. They range from the deeply practical to the utterly bizarre. The pressures of public performance are such that almost anything can come into play as musicians find their best ways to manage nerves, channel energy, calm down, psych up or perhaps seek comfort in routine while preparing to bare their souls to an audience of thousands.

Perhaps the most notorious ritualiser of all was the pianist Shura Cherkassky. One orchestral manager remembers having to wash Cherkassky's hands for him in warm water before a concert. Other legends include his insistence that someone gave him a kiss just before he went on stage: according to a piano technician who worked with him, the backstage area would clear rapidly as start-time approached.

Dame Myra Hess, the British pianist who founded the National Gallery lunchtime concerts during the Blitz, quietly suffered severe pre-performance nerves. She carried with her a pack of cards and would play patience for half an hour prior to a concert, seemingly to focus, calm and distract her mind – and woe betide anybody who interrupted.

The case of Sviatoslav Richter is far more startling. In Bruno Monsaingeon's book *Sviatoslav Richter: Notebooks and Conversations*, the legendary Russian

pianist describes a period of chronic depression that he suffered in 1974: 'It was impossible for me to live without a plastic lobster that I took with me everywhere, leaving it behind only at the very moment I went on stage,' he wrote.

'Nerves', 'stage fright', 'performance anxiety' – call it what you like – but going on stage in front of thousands of people who have high expectations of you is a terrifying prospect. Some musicians, though, have learnt psychological tricks to prevent themselves becoming stressed. A colleague tells me that he remembers Daniel Barenboim rising early on the morning of a concert in order to cook a curry for friends before heading off for his day's work rehearsing and then performing two gargantuan piano concertos. Sakari Oramo, Chief Conductor of the BBC Symphony Orchestra, says that for him, too, the best thing is simply to treat concert day like any other. 'It helps with concentration,'

he says. 'I am not a person for rituals. I just need a good night's sleep, a walk outside and proper nourishment – that's it.'

Sometimes what appears eccentric to others can be in reality a means of effective preparation. The violinist Jascha Heifetz apparently used to ready himself for concerts according to the likely temperature of the hall. If it was known to be hot, he would practise for a couple of days beforehand wearing layers of warm clothing and with the heating on; if cold, the garb would be underwear, with open windows to ensure a chilly draught. This might have looked peculiar, but it made some sense. A more appealing experience attended the flautist Marcel Moyse, who reportedly liked a hearty meal with a glass of wine just before a performance, the idea being that it warmed up the lips.

Alcohol is a tricky area, its effects ranging from Dutch courage to possible disaster. The story goes of two contrasting tenors of bygone days – one a teetotaller, the other rarely without a drink in his hand – who encountered each other backstage in an opera house. The first said to the second: 'How can you go on stage and drink?' The second responded: 'How can you go on stage and *not* drink?'

The tenor Stuart Skelton says that avoiding alcohol is his one big rule before a show. 'Some of my colleagues give me a terrible time over it, but for me it's necessary,' he says. 'There's no real medical reason not to drink unless it affects you, but I find alcohol is drying to my voice. Even if other people say

they can't hear a difference, I notice a change in the amount of energy required if I've had even one beer in that time, so I just stay away from it. Of course, after the performance I break the rule – unless there's another performance within the next 72 hours. During an opera run I'm dry for some time.'

Yoga is a more popular prop: it stretches everything, warms the body and calms the mind. Unexpected encounters with it, however, can prove briefly unsettling. Ted Heath, long before he became the UK's Prime Minister in 1970, went into a dressing room minutes before a concert by the Busch Quartet, only to discover one member of the ensemble balancing there in a headstand.

You won't find the violinist Patricia Kopatchinskaja doing that. 'On the day of a concert, as far as possible I do, physically, *nothing*,' she says. 'It's a day to recharge. I play the general rehearsal, but otherwise I don't move at all. I cannot have phone calls, I cannot read, I cannot think about anything but the piece. I have to become the piece. It's really a concentration thing: I imagine being in that music, telling that story.

'I imagine myself as a storm in the evening. I must collect all this strength and energy and the ability to throw fire into the audience, into the orchestra – to become a storm. You must become a superhuman on stage: you're in the moment and you have no second chances – you cannot repeat something – and to be able to tell a story you must be able to endure it. Becoming

Go, figurine!: two of Grieg's good-luck trinkets, on view at Troldhaugen, the Edvard Grieg museum in Bergen

Under the shell: a 1974 letter from the pianist Sviatoslav Richter in which he introduces his plastic lobster: 'She now sits before me … and is helping me.'

a storm means that you have also to survive in this storm yourself.'

Singers' pre-performance routines vary enormously: some refuse to talk at all, but Skelton says that he tries to speak quietly through the course of the day. Warming up, he remarks, depends on the repertoire: 'If you're singing a Wagner opera that's five hours long and you've warmed up before Act 1, you'll be tired by Act 3.' Fastening the cufflinks also counts for something: 'I have two pairs that I alternate – one is a Britten–Pears pair with Ben and Peter [the composer and tenor duo, partners in music and life] in black relief on a blue background – and the other is a pair of infinity cufflinks that my wife bought me for our wedding.'

It all sounds perfectly rational – except, potentially, the shoes. 'I tend not to put my shoes on till the last minute,' Skelton says. 'I'll be three-quarters dressed, in my costume and ready to go, but I'm still just in my socks. I don't know why that is, but I've always done it. I don't know whether it's superstition or just a way to stay comfortable a little while longer.'

Proms performers, this is your five-minute call … and don't forget to stroke the frog! ●

Jessica Duchen's music journalism has appeared in The Independent, The Guardian and BBC Music Magazine. She is the author of five novels, two plays, biographies of Fauré and Korngold and the libretto for Roxanna Panufnik's opera Silver Birch. Her classical music blog JDCMB has run since 2004.

Sakari Oramo features on 27 August & 11 September; Patricia Kopatchinskaja on 28 August; and Stuart Skelton on 11 September

Getting into the Zone

Icelandic pianist Víkingur Ólafsson (14 August) describes his own routine for arriving on stage in top form

In the days preceding a concert, even if I've played the repertoire before, I will work late into the night, often until 11.00pm or 12 midnight. The goal is always to do the best performance that you have ever done, and that means you work excessively to prepare for it.

I find that, by really practising more than I need to, I can enjoy more freedom on stage and new ideas can be born more spontaneously.

On the morning of the performance, I try to sleep until maybe 9.00am and then I might work two or three hours in the morning, hopefully at the venue, working with the piano (and the piano technician – a very underrated person!) and also adjusting to the hall's acoustic. Then, often, I leave the hall and do some mental practice. If there's time, I'll go through every piece in the concert note by note, in my head, hearing it exactly as I want it to be, in slow motion. That's really hard to do but it brings a kind of confidence.

Like many, I sometimes have nightmares before a concert. My first was the night before my debut with the Iceland Symphony Orchestra when I was 16 and I was playing Tchaikovsky's First Piano Concerto. I dreamt that, while I was playing, the piano – which was right on the edge of the stage – crashed into the audience, and I woke up in a sweat. But other times I might get a nightmare before a big debut, where you're about to go on stage and you have no idea what you're supposed to play, or where the venue has announced a completely different concerto to the one you've prepared.

If I can, I'll sleep for an hour in the afternoon before a concert – just to let the subconscious take over – then I shower and change. That makes it feel like a new day and gives me extra energy.

Many people can't eat before playing, but I'm the opposite. I always have some protein, perhaps a chicken salad, or even some carbohydrates – especially if I'm playing a long recital or a big concerto.

Generally (touch wood!) I don't get nervous: the key is knowing that I have prepared as much as possible, mentally and physically.

It all goes back to always trying to give the best performance you have ever given and finding that relationship between freedom and discipline. You prepare and make all the decisions beforehand in order to be able to forget every one of them on stage and to just go with what's happening in that moment.

Help Musicians

Let the Music
Play On

Please consider leaving a legacy or donate now to let the music you love play on.

Visit helpmusicians.org.uk/donate to find out how you can support today.

Love Music: Help Musicians

Photo credit: Antonio Zazueta Olmos

" *Help Musicians was there when I needed them at the start of my career and in the last year alone they've helped 19,000 musicians with financial support when the pandemic destroyed their earnings.*

For the last 100 years the charity has been providing help in times of crisis and opportunity, thanks to the generosity of donors past and present. Help us make a difference to the lives of future talented musicians across the UK.

Natalya Romaniw
Soprano & Help Musicians Ambassador

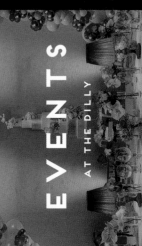

Zurich International Orchestra Series 2021-22

Orchestras and soloists from around the world perform in the intimate setting of Cadogan Hall.

Full details coming soon:
cadoganhall.com/zios

Join our mailing list to be kept up to date:
cadoganhall.com/join

Cadogan Hall
Sloane Terrace
London
SW1X 9DQ

ZURICH®

CADOGAN HALL

I am music

I live through your moments

Your first shake of the rattle

Your recorder lesson

Your match day anthem

Your queueing anticipation

Your hands in the air

Your main stage mayhem

Your favourite movie scene

Your first dance

Your family singalong

Your standing ovation

Your swan song.

The Haberdashers' Aske's Boys' School

Nurturing Excellence

Music at Habs

Habs provides a platform for some of the nation's most exciting and exceptional young musicians. Taking pride in our diverse and progressive cultural programme, we offer the perfect environment for students to refine and develop their passion. Nurturing the voice of each individual is at the heart of our approach and we are proud of our heritage of furthering the most remarkable young artists. Our state-of-the-art facilities, performance opportunities, and an inspirational faculty make this the ideal home for the talented and driven young mind.

Music scholarships available

Perform regularly at the Barbican Centre

Co-located with Habs Girls

5+, 7+, 11+, 13+ and 16+ applications now open for September 2022 entry

Visit us virtually: www.virtualvisit.habsboys.org.uk

Website: www.habsboys.org.uk

Musician, Muse, Motivator

NATASHA LOGES celebrates Pauline Viardot – the singer, composer and society figure born 200 years ago – whose musical gifts and personal charm inspired a plethora of musical and literary luminaries in 19th-century Europe

orn in Paris in 1821, Pauline Viardot (née García) was an extraordinarily gifted, all-round musician whose career took her across Europe during the latter half of the 19th century. Although primarily a mezzo-soprano, she was also an excellent pianist, sought-after teacher and innovative composer. She was steeped in music from her childhood, thanks to her parents, the Spanish tenor Manuel García and soprano María Joaquina Sitches. Her siblings, Maria Malibran and Manuel García the younger, were also successful singers.

Pauline hoped to become a pianist but, following her father's death when she was 10 years old, her mother insisted on a vocal career. She made her professional debut aged 16 in Brussels; two years later, she made her London debut singing Desdemona in Rossini's *Otello* and thereafter sang in every London season from 1848 to 1858. Nevertheless, she remained proficient enough to give her first concert as a pianist, accompany herself in her own songs, play piano duets with Chopin and Clara Schumann, and read and sing the full score of Berlioz's opera *The Trojans* from the piano, to his admiration.

Aged 18, she married Louis Viardot, who was director of Paris's Théâtre Italien. Although he was 20 years older, they enjoyed a happy, mutually rewarding marriage. He offered unstinting support, relinquishing his work to manage her career. When they were apart, she wrote affectionate daily letters to her 'dear little Loulou', which testify to their companionship. He accepted her many admirers, including the Russian writer Ivan Turgenev, whom she met in the 1840s. Turgenev was devoted to her, often living with or near her in an unconventional *ménage à trois*.

Viardot's three-octave vocal range and compelling histrionic qualities – along with her knowledge of Spanish, French, Italian, English, German and Russian – dazzled many composers. She created the role of Fidès in Meyerbeer's *Le prophète*, singing it more than 200 times across Europe; Meyerbeer recalled that Viardot 'rose to tragic heights such as I have never seen in the theatre before'. Gounod wrote the title-role of his opera *Sapho* for her; Berlioz was besotted with her, calling her 'one of the greatest artists ... in the past and present history of music', and considered – but ultimately rejected – her as Dido in *The Trojans*. Brahms persuaded her to interrupt her retirement to sing the premiere of his *Alto Rhapsody* in 1870; and in 1873 she sang the premiere of Massenet's oratorio *Marie-Magdeleine*. In 1877 Saint-Saëns – who described her voice as 'superhuman rather than human' – dedicated *Samson and Delilah* to her but, aged 56, she declined the role.

Viardot also excelled in historic roles, including Orpheus in Berlioz's 1859 version of Gluck's *Orphée et Eurydice*.

She had a lifelong affinity with Mozart's *Don Giovanni*, alternating the roles of Donna Anna and Zerlina on stages from London to Prague. She recalled being backstage, aged 4, during a performance in which her father and sister were singing: the Commendatore terrified her. The autograph manuscript of the opera was among her most treasured possessions.

> Viardot's three-octave vocal range and compelling histrionic qualities – along with her knowledge of Spanish, French, Italian, English, German and Russian – dazzled many composers.

Her extensive correspondence offers a glimpse into the precarious lives of freelance musicians. When Viardot travelled, she did not always have a contract, but might have to arrange performances upon her arrival, exercise tact with local singers and compete with rival prima donnas. She thrived on her audience's adoration, noting in letters how often she was recalled to the stage.

Wherever the Viardots were, they hosted private, often lavish, musical gatherings. Pauline's Thursday-evening salon in Paris was the scene for many informal concerts with close friends, such as the novelist George Sand and her companion Chopin, admiring colleagues such as Gounod and

▲ Pauline Viardot, whom the music critic Henry Chorley described as 'unusual, exotic'; 1842 portrait by Timofey Andreyevich Neff

Liszt, and illustrious visitors such as Charles Dickens and Alfred de Musset.

Viardot had always collaborated actively on the music written for her; however, her own composition blossomed after she retired from the stage in her early forties. Her husband's republican convictions made it too hot for them in the Second Empire, so in 1863 they fled to Baden-Baden. In this delightful millionaires' playground, she built an art gallery in her garden and a small opera house where dramatic works could be performed by her social circle and the various singers who flocked to her for lessons. In those years she composed three chamber operas to librettos by Turgenev: *Trop de femmes*, *L'ogre* and *Le dernier sorcier* – playful, fantastical works in which her female pupils and children could participate. *Le dernier sorcier* attracted high praise from the music critic Henry Chorley, and Liszt declared her a 'woman composer of genius'. *Le dernier sorcier* was performed in Weimar in 1869 and Riga and Karlsruhe the following year, albeit reorchestrated thickly by Eduard Lassen and translated into rather lumpen German. The work later vanished, to be rediscovered only in 2005.

Viardot wrote approximately 100 songs. Her favoured poets included contemporaries, such as Turgenev, Musset, Gautier and Mörike, and great predecessors such as Pushkin and Goethe. The songs best capture her cosmopolitanism, including German lieder, popular Italian songs, French *mélodies* and a Russian album. Her

profound understanding of the capabilities of both voice and piano is clear, as well as her instinct for drama and narrative. In response to the text, her melodies and keyboard textures are greatly varied and often technically demanding. Like Liszt (but generally more pithily), she fused the best and most innovative aspects of contemporary German and French music, favouring original trajectories and colours that take the listener across Europe.

Alongside these original works, Viardot's arrangements of instrumental works as songs attained staggering popularity. For instance, her transcriptions of 12 of Chopin's Mazurkas, with words by Louis Pomey, were widely performed; the composer himself highly approved of them. Such cross-fertilisation between genres was widespread: Liszt, for instance, made numerous popular keyboard arrangements of Schubert's songs. Viardot drew on much-loved works such as Schubert's waltzes or Brahms's *Hungarian Dances* for such creations.

After the 1870 defeat of Napoleon III in the Franco-Prussian War, Viardot returned to Paris, teaching and hosting her salon. Her circle now embraced figures including Tchaikovsky, Fauré and Massenet, to whom she appeared very much a *grande dame* of music. She also resumed composition in her old age, producing two more chamber operas to her own librettos: *Le conte de fées* (1879) and *Cendrillon* (1904). A short opera with dialogue, written when Viardot was 83, the latter is a light-hearted and graceful retelling of Perrault's *Cinderella* tale,

with a bumbling, comic stepfather replacing the evil stepmother.

Viardot's students included some of the most successful singers of the next generation, such as Désirée Artôt, Aglaja Orgeni, Marianne Brandt and Antoinette Sterling. She published a manual on singing; an album of selected songs and arias with detailed comments on phrasing, accentuation and interpretation; and a critical edition of a selection of Schubert's lieder. These give us detailed insights into professional vocal technique and performance during the 19th century.

Perhaps unsurprisingly, Viardot's four children were successful musicians in turn, including her daughter, the composer Louise Héritte. Viardot remained an admired and influential figure until her death in 1910, aged 88. Although she is now remembered mainly as a singer, she exerted considerable influence on her musical and literary milieu. Apart from her collaborations with leading composers, her beautifully crafted compositions offer fascinating insights into her glittering world and reveal an overlooked but unique creative voice. ●

Natasha Loges is Head of Postgraduate Programmes and Professor of Musicology at the Royal College of Music, London. Also an author and pianist, she appears on BBC Radio 3's *Record Review* and writes for BBC Music Magazine.

Pauline Viardot and Her Circle
P@CH 6 • 6 SEPTEMBER

See Index for works by Viardot's friends and colleagues: Bizet, Brahms & Saint-Saëns

Secrets in the Void

As we emerge from the extended quelling of
music-making by the coronavirus pandemic, author and broadcaster
WILL SELF considers how an encounter with John Cage's infamous
4'33" has made him think afresh about the ways in which sound and
silence bring each other to life

thought I'd attended a performance of John Cage's infamous 4'33" fairly recently – and I'm not just speaking in that figurative way that so annoys younger people, although I concede I can be guilty of that. ('The other day' being, as my adult children never cease to point out, a sort of paternal – and quite likely paternalistic – uchronia: an era that never really was, within which the sands of time revolve anticlockwise and counter-intuitively.) But perhaps the feeling I have that it was only yesterday when, in 2011, I saw the pianist of the ensemble Apartment House walk onto the stage of London's Queen Elizabeth Hall, sit down at the instrument, open its lid, then remain there, mute for four minutes and 33 seconds, is a function not of my amnesia, but of the piece's inherent amusia.

By which I mean to say that one thing Cage's audacious piece leads us to consider is that music does not subsist in a realm it creates for itself but, rather, it comes into being out of silence. I remember having a conversation with a friend who's a theoretical physicist about the fundamental constituents of matter. Speaking of the Big Bang, he remarked on how subatomic particles 'emerged out of the void'; to which I retorted, 'But nothing will come of nothing.' 'Scientist my friend may be, but he's also a Shakespearean, so he got the reference to King Lear and

snapped back: 'On the contrary, *everything* comes of nothing.'

With no internal temporal structure born of the regular succession of notes and chords; no harmonic structure born of notes and chords, their alterations of pitch and timbre; and with no succession of notes to form melodies, 4'33" is arguably that most curious of things: a musical piece in which the experience of music as we conventionally understand it is impossible. The Guardian reviewer of the performance I witnessed in 2011 was reduced to descanting on 'a considerable wind solo from the stomach of someone behind me'. To this, and also to a bizarre solecism, describing the rendition of the piece as 'surprisingly brisk'.

No, with no time of its own – beyond its overall length – 4'33" gets lost in the greater and more tenebrous silence of the poorly recalled past. I like to think that, preparatory to the pianist coming on stage and the lights dimming, I experienced that enjoyable frisson – well known to the regular concert-goer – as my ears, accustomed to the background hubbub of conversation and mastication, began to sense a growing soundlessness. This positive-feedback loop – whereby sections of an audience semi-consciously register those around them falling silent and do so as well, thereby precipitating a mounting cascade of quietness – is arguably as important for establishing the integrity of the performance that follows as is the silent tocsin of the conductor's baton tapping the air.

What, then, can it have been like to experience the massing silence prior to 4'33"? Was it some kind of aural *mise en abyme*, calling the audience's attention not to the music of the spheres, but to their absolute quietude as they revolve in a vacuum quite unable to act as a medium for sound-waves? I can only restate what I've said above in a different way: while, in my memory, the decade that's elapsed since that evening at the Queen Elizabeth Hall has an indeterminate quality – the events piled into it either bunched together or drawn out – the collective consciousness of it is more than amply notated.

> 66 Music does not subsist in a realm it creates for itself but, rather, it comes into being out of silence. 99

Another way of thinking about this is to use the philosopher Henri Bergson's distinction between clock time and our more fluid personal experience of duration. Clock time is a necessary standardisation – indeed, it exists purely as a consensus between individuals to mutually agree the 'position' of events in space–time. Duration, by contrast, is a wholly subjective phenomenon – the best evocation of this that I know being the character of Dunbar in Joseph Heller's antiwar novel Catch-22. A young American airman, facing likely and imminent death, Dunbar notes that every

▲ Light in the dark (or vice versa): the vast rotunda of the Pantheon in Rome

if only semi-consciously – many of the most fundamental terms of our existence: are we in the world of others or are we fundamentally alone? Is our own life temporally bound or transcendent? Can we view ourselves *sub specie aeternitatis* or not? Is there an Immortal Beloved or only a series of contingent amours? Moreover, I think it possible that this alternation between fermata and fanfare is not only the origin of the intense emotionality of music, but also explains its curious singularity as opposed to the other arts: namely, its non-representational quality. (Unless, that is, you think Mozart's flutes really do sound like bird song, and Strauss's horns like the föhn.)

This oft-remarked-upon aspect of music is what – at least superficially – renders it so puzzling, at least to those prosaic souls who believe they know the evolutionary cost of everything, but arguably the value of nothing. The argument goes that music confers no obvious adaptive advantage on the individual, unlike the symbolic art forms that correlate so well with all manner of real-life skills. So what's the point of it? Certainly, in my own field, novels can be placed on a sort of spectrum between those that – very loosely – tell us where the food is, and those that call upon us to consider the nature (and possibly the whereabouts) of God or gods. The analogy here might be between those visual artworks that are mimetic (they show) and those that are diegetic (they tell). My view is that the distinction, in all art forms, is apparent rather than real – there's a lurking quality of what-it's-aboutness

hour he experiences bored seems to last appreciably – if not infinitely – longer than those when he's engaged (in combat, for example). Seeking to extend his lifespan, Dunbar actively pursues ennui.

Chamber music: composer John Cage in a soundproofed anechoic room in 1990; a similar experience almost 40 years earlier partly inspired his radical piece 4'33", whose only performance instruction reads 'tacet'. 'There is no such thing as an empty space or an empty time,' Cage said. 'There is always something to see, something to hear. In fact, try as we may to make a silence, we cannot.'

Arguably, this is what every composer and musician aims at as well: but not boredom, rather the intense engagement that comes when, in shifting from our personal sense of duration to the communal one of incremental time, all manner of feelings are sparked into being. It's easy to see why this motion – which I think of as having the almost frightening inertia of an explosively driven piston – should be so affecting. It stimulates us to consider – even

in all music, no matter how seemingly abstract, not least Cage's 4'33".

The philosopher Lao Tzu compared the relationship between silence and music to that which obtains between a bowl and the hollow space it contains – without this little local void, the bowl simply wouldn't exist. As I say: I believe musicians understand this intuitively – it isn't only the deafening silences interspersing the final six chords of Sibelius's Symphony No. 5 that summon the spirit of the muse Euterpe, it's the alternation between every note and its rest. One way of thinking about this is that each piece of music has a substructure of silences: a palimpsest of the pacific that's abraded by sound, even as the players rub at their strings. We all know those fermatas that we love best – for they occur immediately beside the melodies, the harmonies and the paradiddles we also love best.

And, if music needs always to be considered in relationship to silence, then we must also interrogate the nature of these caesuras – because, of course, they are by no means uniform. Rather, the counterpoint calls our attention to the quietude that has shrouded all musical endeavours since the inception of the coronavirus pandemic: namely the almost universal suspension of live performance. It isn't only that *Guardian* critic who's compelled to fill 4'33" with farts and gurgles – we all do it. We hear the rush of blood in our ears in extreme silence – and the chemical interaction of our digestive acids with our pre-performance snack; we sense the acoustical properties of the

hall we're seated in: the local void that creates Lao Tzu's 'bowl'. Everything does indeed come out of nothing; but this isn't a pure vacuum.

The faint susurrus of the settled audience, the shifting in their seats of the players – these perturb a silence seamed by the distant streaming of traffic along roads, tracks and through the sky. What might it have been like to only hear sounds made by natural things – whether fauna, flora or the weather? The organic feel of classical music – and indeed all music that preceded it – may be a function of just this: the interrelation of interspecific signalling to the accompaniment of rain and wind. All of which is to say, there is never an absolute silence in nature – if there were to be, we'd experience it as a manifest threat. But we're all familiar with this phenomenon, I think: a sudden and unexpected hush as the fridge's thermostat shuts off its pump or the pneumatic drill five streets away stops. In such moments we feel, paradoxically, an acute *presence* of sound – not without reason do we succumb to the cliché of a 'deafening silence'.

Douglas Mawson, leader of the Australasian Antarctic Expedition of 1911–14, noted the eeriness of this phenomenon when it's a force 12 hurricane that suddenly abates. 'On such occasions the auditory sense was strangely affected [and] the habitual droning of many weeks would still reverberate in the ears.' Left alone for months in an isolated hut while the other members of his party were out sledging, Morton Moyes, another of the

66 The philosopher Lao Tzu compared the relationship between silence and music to that which obtains between a bowl and the hollow space it contains – without this little local void, the bowl simply wouldn't exist. 99

explorers, found that 'the silence is so painful now that I have a continual singing in my left ear, much like a barrel organ, only it's the same tune all the time'.

A fresh kind of hell, indeed – and it may well be one that we all inhabit. For the sounds and the soundlessness that surround us now are for the most part quite as mechanically repetitive as a barrel organ with a single tune. It's this, I imagine, that inspires people to upload videos to YouTube showing them 'playing' Cage's piece on a microwave oven – or indeed a fridge. Arguably we're all composers of *musique concrète* now: artfully arranging the workaday sounds that surround us so as to block out yet more annoying quotidian ones. Blanketing it all is the phenomenon known as 'the global hum': a persistent, low-frequency buzzing sound that something like 4 per cent of the Earth's population believe they can hear whenever they concentrate on the kind-of-a-hush that, if not 'all over the world', is certainly what passes for tranquillity in its built-up areas.

If this mysterious noise exists at all in a measurable sense, it may well signal the end of silence as we've heretofore conceived of it. Tinnitus, in which our pernicious use of earphones and our penchant for highly amplified music are heavily implicated, is possibly the personal hum out of which the global one is fabricated. The hiss prior to the onslaught of music mediated by electronic pulses is an aural effect we all experience – plunging us into an

Antarctica of the mind. For my own part, I've experienced mounting amusia – or, at any rate, an antipathy to recorded music – the more I've become aware of ambient sound.

A few years ago I moved into a small flat that turned out to have a generator unit for the corner shop beneath affixed to its outside wall. At irregular intervals this unit would start into buzzing existence. The buzz felt so persistent that, if I inserted the waxiest and most mouldable of earplugs, it seemed as if some microscopic cyborg insect were trapped deep inside my ears – so preternaturally sensitive had I become to the least unwanted noise. I resorted to music to mask this maddening irritation – and here, I suppose, was my downfall; for – in counterpointing the buzz with … well, with much of the music I love, from the icily beautiful harmonies of Sibelius's Fifth to the pellucid atonality of Berg's Piano Sonata – I tainted it by association.

Neuroscience teaches us that we experience the phenomenon of the 'earworm' – that tune we cannot get out of our heads – when our listening is interrupted, leaving us struggling to get to the end. But I'm now afflicted with the earworm of silence, for it's like a performance of Cage's 4′33″ that's been interrupted too many times, such that I cannot get to the end of it and so experience music properly anew. ●

Author, journalist and broadcaster Will Self has written 12 novels (including the Man Booker Prize-shortlisted *Umbrella*, 2012) in addition to short-story collections. His non-fiction titles include the memoir *Will* (2019). He is Professor of Contemporary Thought at Brunel University.

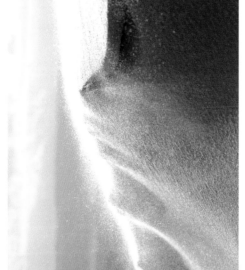

White noise: explorer Douglas Mawson reported how, during his Antarctic expedition of 1911–14, the sudden abatement of howling winds would produce 'a hallucinatory effect' on him and his team

A Gift to the Nation

Historian and broadcaster LUCY WORSLEY tells the story of the Royal Albert Hall, 150 years since it opened as part of Queen Victoria and Prince Albert's grand project to provide cultural enlightenment for the people – and 80 years since it became home to the BBC Proms his year, which marks the Royal Albert Hall's 150th anniversary, is the perfect time to take a look at its history. The home of the Proms since 1941, the building sometimes known as 'the nation's village hall' grew out of a royal relationship that revolved around music and love.

The Hall's foundation stone was laid on 20 May 1867 by Queen Victoria. Six years after the death of her beloved Albert, the widowed queen described the day's events in her diary as most distressing.

Ten thousand people had gathered in an enormous tent erected just south of Kensington Gardens. 'The National Anthem was sung,' Victoria recorded, 'and then came that most trying moment, from which I suffered severely.' She had to read an address, 'full of allusions to my beloved one, which agitated me dreadfully, & I was nearly overcome'. Dressed in black, near to tears, she nevertheless managed to get the construction of the Royal Albert Hall of Arts and Sciences under way. And if you're lucky enough to be sitting in Seat 87, Row 11, in Stalls K of the Hall, you'll find the foundation stone still hidden beneath your seat.

The stone-laying ceremony also saw a piece of music played which had been written by Prince Albert himself. 'How

I thought of dearest Albert's feeling so shy about ever having this composition performed,' his widow wrote, 'which I had helped in writing down for him, & singing the solos for him.' So Victoria herself was a collaborator in the piece!

In describing how they'd worked on it together, Albert coming up with the ideas, Victoria writing them down, she puts her finger on something central to this most famous of royal romances: a shared love of music. But it also shows which one of the two – behind closed doors at least – was really the boss in the relationship. The queen was merely the secretary.

Victoria was very conscious that her husband had 'superior' taste. While her own taste in music was for tunes and melodrama, Albert's was more upmarket. And he made it his mission in life to use noble and worthy music as a means to elevate the souls of British citizens.

Victoria had been born just across the road from the Royal Albert Hall, in Kensington Palace. She was a lonely child, living in what was then a minor and rather ramshackle palace. Her father had died when she was a baby, bequeathing her little but debts. But her great consolation was music. She could lose herself in singing, passionate piano-playing and dressing her tiny dolls in tiny outfits fashioned to represent the opera stars she longed to be taken to see.

When she was 16, though, her first cousin Albert was shipped over from Germany in the expectation that they would fall in love and marry. Which, after some

hesitation, they did. Albert could sense that this would not be the perfect match.

Cerebral Albert liked going to bed early with a good book, whereas Victoria preferred staying up late and waltzing at balls. This new dance, described by Lord Byron as 'the wicked waltz', was scandalising Europe, and Albert did not approve of his wife's sense of fun. One night at dinner, his medical adviser tapped Victoria on the shoulder and quietly informed her that 'a queen does not drink a bottle of wine a day'.

Victoria quite frankly found Handel boring and preferred the catchy dance tunes of Johann Strauss II: 'I am a very modern person,' she claimed. Albert's preference, though, was for the staider pleasures of German lieder, the poetic songs enjoyed by Europe's middle classes, performed not in the opera house, but in the respectable context of the family drawing room. His favourite composer was Felix Mendelssohn, who visited Buckingham Palace to play and sing with Victoria and Albert. And, when it came to the concert hall, Albert was in the audience when the Philharmonic Society of London performed the British premiere of Mendelssohn's 'Scottish' Symphony in 1842.

As he and Victoria had more and more children, Albert embarked upon a project to improve the British, to bring his wife's subjects up to his own higher standards.

He began to conceive of a Great Exhibition, known in full as 'The Great Exhibition of the Works of Industry of

▲ A monument to the arts and sciences, and to Victoria's love for Albert, after whom she named it: the opening ceremony of the Royal Albert Hall, on 29 March 1871, witnessed by a crowd of 10,000

All Nations'. Situated in Hyde Park and housed in the famous 'Crystal Palace', an enormous greenhouse designed by gardener and architect Joseph Paxton, it was to feature scientific, industrial and artistic products of all kinds. Prizes awarded to the best ones would create a healthy spirit of competition.

800 sang Handel's 'Hallelujah' Chorus. And, despite the doubts that had been expressed at such an ambitious and righteous project, the exhibition was a commercial success. The sources of profit included some of London's first paying toilets: the cost to visitors of using them would give rise to the expression 'spending a penny'.

Albert's exhibition was organised with the help of the energetic administrator Henry Cole. When work got mired in detail, Albert is supposed to have demanded: 'We must have steam: get Cole!' And their Great Exhibition created a great legacy – a huge sum of money (£186,000) that was more than enough to purchase 96 acres of prime land in South Kensington upon which to build further improving projects: the Victoria & Albert Museum, the Science Museum, the Natural History Museum, Imperial College and the Royal College of Art, as well as the Royal Albert Hall and the Royal College of Music. This new cultural quarter of London, with Exhibition Road as its thoroughfare, became known as 'Albertopolis'.

Albert was clearly a brilliant man, a polymath and an important force for social change and education in Britain. But, in many ways, he pursued his own interests and workaholic tendencies at the expense of the confidence and *joie de vivre* of his wife. Slowly, under his disapproving gaze, she abandoned the enjoyments of her youth. Whenever they had one of their not-infrequent quarrels, Albert's practice was to walk out, go to his own room and write her a letter telling her why she was wrong.

The royal family (including Victoria and Albert) surrounded by the Archbishop of Canterbury and other dignitaries in the Crystal Palace at the opening of the Great Exhibition on 1 May 1851 (painting by Henry Courtney Selous, 1803–90)

The exhibits included a large selection of musical instruments, such as the new range of horns fashioned from brass by one Adolphe Sax, who gave his name to the saxophone.

When Albert's wife opened his Great Exhibition on 1 May 1851, a choir of

Yet she undoubtedly loved him and, after Albert's unexpected death in 1861 at the age of just 42, she described herself as 'all alone, desolate and broken-hearted'. His influence even persisted from beyond the grave, causing her to make one of the very few public appearances of her early widowhood to lay that foundation stone of the Royal Albert Hall in his honour.

Designed by Lieutenant Colonel H. Y. D. Scott of the Royal Engineers, the Hall was an incredible feat of engineering, roughly inspired by the ancient Roman amphitheatres of Arles and Nîmes. An architectural model was made – still kept in the Hall's archives today – which has a gap where the floor of the Arena should be. You could poke up your head through the round hole to get a panoramic, if miniature, view of what the auditorium was going to be like.

The finished Hall's roof of iron and glass weighed more than 600 tonnes. The building was intended for gatherings of all kinds, including conferences, speeches and exhibitions. But, when it came to concerts, it turned out that the acoustic was terrible. That glass roof had to have a huge piece of canvas slung beneath it in order to improve the sound. Yet the Hall was visually magnificent. And it also had an enormous organ, nicknamed the 'Voice of Jupiter', which was powered by two steam engines. The organ's pipes, if laid end to end, would extend for nine miles.

When Queen Victoria returned to South Kensington to open the finished Hall

The Voice of Jupiter

GRAEME KAY explores the history of the Royal Albert Hall's mighty Willis organ

'The organ sounded like the Voice of Jupiter. The audience was left breathless and tingling.' So wrote a critic in the 1960s. Certainly, there's nothing quite like the sound of these 9,999 pipes – in sizes ranging from the length of a pencil to a 42-ft (12.8m) behemoth weighing nearly a tonne – in full cry.

When the Royal Albert Hall opened in 1871, the organ had already been five years in the planning; Henry Cole had appointed the celebrated organ-builder Henry Willis to the task. The Hall's size demanded an instrument that would make it, for many years, the largest in the world.

The first full recital was given on 18 July 1871 by Britain's most famous concert organist, W. T. Best. A procession of distinguished international musicians followed him, including the composer Camille Saint-Saëns, as well as Anton Bruckner, who was credited with playing

loudly enough to cause the two steam engines that provided the wind supply to run out of puff.

Building on improvements made by Harrison & Harrison in 1924 and 1933, the firm of N. P. Mander undertook a two-year, £1.5m restoration in 2002 – disposing of scores of tennis balls and other junk that had found its way into the pipes, while also stopping the famously wheezing bellows from leaking.

The organ's earth-shaking sound has not been the exclusive preserve of classical concerts and the Proms. Simon Preston recorded Bach's Toccata in D minor on it for the opening titles of the film *Rollerball*; Wendy Carlos used it in the score for *Tron*; it's heard in Pink Floyd's 'Autumn '68' and Muse's 'Megalomania'; and there are faint echoes of Frank Zappa using the organ in 'Louie Louie' recorded at a live concert in 1967.

New York-based British organist David Briggs was part of the inaugural concert, post-restoration: 'The organ exudes almost limitless swathes of colour,' he says, 'from the merest whisper to a *tutti* that would cause any self-respecting orchestra to fall into surrender.' Famously, because of the Hall's crowded schedule, lone organists often have to practise and record during the night: 'I finally got on the organ at 3.40am,' adds Briggs, 'and then the cleaning started at 5.00am. But the vacuum cleaners didn't stand a chance!'

Graeme Kay is an organ-lover and a digital platforms producer for BBC Radio 3 and Radio 4.

A Gift to the Nation

Jimi Hendrix and Pink Floyd standing out among the artists who have performed there. Victoria would also have enjoyed the ballet, *Cirque du Soleil*, opera, indeed every imaginable kind of performance – both professional and amateur – that fills the building (pandemics aside) up to 400 times a year. The extrovert, extravagant spirit of Queen Victoria fills the Hall alongside the emphasis on quality and education supported by her nerdy husband.

on 29 March 1871, her diary recorded how 'Good Mr Cole' (he was by then Director of the Victoria & Albert Museum down the road) 'was quite crying with emotion & delight'.

Another feature of Albertopolis would be a new Royal College of Music. When Albert had come to Britain to marry Victoria in 1841, the country had lacked a strong school of native composers. So it was that Albert's German favourites – Beethoven and Mendelssohn, or Italians such as Rossini – had formed the core of the concerts at court. By the time Queen Victoria died in 1901, though, his efforts and establishments such as the Royal College had meant that British composers, Edward Elgar and Hubert Parry among them, were able to make the grade internationally. But, in many ways, what goes on in the Royal Albert Hall today reflects Victoria's more exuberant and catholic enjoyment of music than Albert's.

It's also worth remembering that the Hall isn't just for concerts – it has an important place in political history too. In 1912 it was the venue for perhaps Emmeline Pankhurst's most memorable speech, the first she gave after getting out of prison for law-breaking in support of female suffrage. 'We women suffragists have a great mission …' she told her supporters. 'It is to free half the human race.'

For some years after his death, like many people scarred by trauma, Victoria had found that listening to music aroused unbearably painful emotions. Gradually, though, as she regained her confidence in ruling by herself, rather than just doing what Albert told her to do, she began once again to indulge her own eclectic tastes. These included not only Wagner, but also Gilbert and Sullivan, and the music of the Indian composer Rabindranath Tagore.

And she would have approved of the way her husband's Hall has grown just as famous for its performances of pop as of classical music, with Bob Dylan,

And then, in 1943, the AGM of the Women's Institute, held at the Royal Albert Hall, resolved that equal work deserved equal pay. A certain Mrs Green put it to the members that 'women are important, not just important as housewives and mothers and girlfriends and "sewers-on-of-buttons" but vital and essential if we are to win this war'. It would actually take until 1970 for the Equal Pay Act finally to be passed, but the Women's Institute returned to the Hall in 2015 to celebrate its centenary.

Yet perhaps the best-known association with the Royal Albert Hall is that of the Proms, a series of concerts set

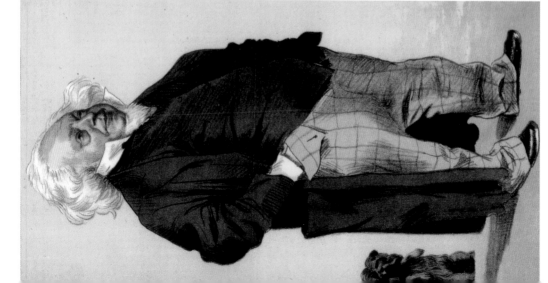

'We need steam: get Cole!': Henry Cole, civil servant, educational campaigner and the organising force behind Prince Albert's Great Exhibition of 1851, the profits of which led to the building of the Royal Albert Hall as part of the 'Albertopolis' cultural quarter in London's South Kensington (caricature in *Vanity Fair*, August 1871)

up very much in line with Prince Albert's ambitions.

Robert Newman was the manager of the Queen's Hall off Regent Street, the original home of the Proms. When he devised the first series of concerts in 1895, he had a clear manifesto for what he wanted to do. 'Mr Robert Newman's Promenade Concerts', as he called them, were to be 'nightly concerts to train the public in easy stages, popular at first, gradually raising the standard until I have created a public for classical and modern music.' The series was taken over by the BBC in 1927, and in 1941, after the Queen's Hall was destroyed in an air raid, the Proms settled into a new and lasting home at the Royal Albert Hall.

For its 150th birthday, the building inspired by the aspirations of the Great Exhibition has acquired a Great Excavation: an underground café, archive and meeting space.

Should they visit the Hall 150 years after its opening, the ghosts of both lowbrow Queen Victoria and highbrow Prince Albert would find lots to enjoy. ●

Lucy Worsley is a broadcaster, historian and author who has presented over 40 programmes and mini-series for the BBC, including Mozart's London Odyssey, Tales from the Royal Wardrobes and Royal Palace Secrets. Among her books are Queen Victoria: Daughter, Wife, Mother, Widow and the children's titles My Name Is Victoria and The Austen Girls. She is Chief Curator at Historic Royal Palaces.

See Index for anniversary commissions by Britta Byström, Grace Evangeline Mason and Augusta Read Thomas; see Season Overview for organ recitals on 1 August and 4 September

Tailor-Made Sounds

Four ways in which the Proms has made novel use of the RAH's unique spaces

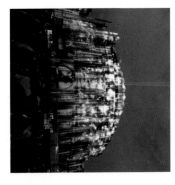

All the Hall's a Stage

A Late Night Prom in 2014 saw what *The Times* called 'a happening of epic zaniness'. Benedict Mason's *meld* dispersed players and singers into practically every crevice of the Hall. Performers processed in the Gallery, encircled the audience from Grand Tier boxes, played in the Arena and roamed in the aisles. Even the corridors around the auditorium were used in a site-specific performance that not so much took place in the Royal Albert Hall as set its whole fabric resonating from within.

Kissin in the Round

The first ever solo piano recital at the Proms, in 1997, placed the 25-year-old Russian wunderkind Evgeny Kissin right in the centre of the Royal Albert Hall's oval Arena. Sitting at his Steinway, encircled by the Prommers, he gave a virtuoso performance that evoked the spectacle and drama of a gladiatorial event. He clearly relished the occasion, treating the audience to eight encores.

Cosmic Voices from On High

Gustav Holst's astrological suite *The Planets* has been a favourite at the Proms since Malcolm Sargent first conducted it at the festival in 1951. Since then there have been more than 50 performances. The cavernous Royal Albert Hall auditorium is the perfect space for the vast scale and cinematic impact of Holst's score. The suite's final movement, 'Neptune, the Mystic' is a high point in more ways than one. The female chorus of heavenly voices is placed in the upper reaches of the Gallery, with the singers gradually retreating backstage to create the effect of fading magically into the ether.

A Living Canvas

In 2018 *Five Telegrams* launched the Proms's celebrations to mark 100 years since the end of the First World War. Inspired by modes of wartime communication — telegrams, codes, ciphers, printed propaganda — composer Anna Meredith and design/production company 59 Productions collaborated on a work in which 3D light projections (pictured *above*) animated the Hall's exterior and interior. It was a vast project for an all-embracing building. 'We've been as bold with this piece as we can be,' said Meredith.

Plunder Enlightening

Is there such a thing as a truly original work? Radio 3's **TOM SERVICE** explores how composers have copied, borrowed and quoted from each other for centuries, and how the transfer of ideas is fundamental to the act of creativity

ou'll often read how a composer's value in the annals of music history is directly proportional to their originality; as if their quality of original, never-imagined-before brilliance sets them apart from all the rest and assures them their place in the pantheon. And it follows that, if you're the opposite of original – if instead you're a composer or musician involved in copying, remodelling, plagiarising, stealing or borrowing – you're disqualified from your position on the pedestal.

All of those (non-original) words don't merely suggest alternative musical practices to the business of being unique and one-off, they are words that carry unethical undertones: if we're stealing and remaking, we're doing something that goes against the very principles of honest artistic creation, and we're engaged in activities that will put us on the wrong side of the law. Literally: Ed Sheeran,

Pharrell Williams, Men at Work and dozens of other musicians and bands have been involved in court cases, accused of copying and stealing other people's work without the right clearances, often with financially enormous consequences.

It's a field day for lawyers and, from the perspective of classical music culture, it's possible to look askance at all that litigious courtroom drama in pop music as having nothing to do with all of the original-and-best composers who make up the canons of the classical and the programmes of the Proms.

Except, that's not true. At all. Because, if copyright law had been around in 18th-century Germany and Austria, Johann Sebastian Bach, George Frideric Handel, Wolfgang Amadeus Mozart – and all the rest – would have been found guilty of plagiarism, pilfery, passing other composers' work off as their own and engaging in acts of copyright-infringing

delinquency. That might seem a shocking idea but, when you listen to Mozart stealing from Handel's *Messiah* in his *Requiem*, or think of how Bach nicks so many tunes for his own purposes, from Vivaldi to Hassler, or how Handel passes off cobbled-together bits and pieces of his back catalogue as new works, you'll hear how all of them are involved in dodgy creative activities that would have landed them in a copyright courtroom drama in pop music the same offences today. And yet what's most shocking of all isn't that this kind of reworking is common to those composers, but that it's endemic to the fabric of every note and every work of classical music.

In fact, the real crime isn't the stealing or the borrowing that these composers are up to – it's the idea that originality is the *sine qua non* of the music we should value the most. The truth is, without remaking, copying and creative thievery, none of the music of this year's Proms programme could have been composed.

The fetish of originality is an original sin of the classical music canon: it's a convenient music-historical fiction that's told to mask a much messier and more uncomfortable truth: that to compose isn't necessarily to come up with anything original at all, but to put together what's already there. You can do that in new ways – you can make chains of ideas and combinations of sounds and surfaces and structures that have never been heard before – but your material will almost always come from somewhere else, from sounds that already exist in the world. Which leads to the paradoxical truism that you can't be 'original' without stealing, without remodelling, without referencing and remaking.

And, to prove my case for the essential un-originality of so much of the music we love dearly, let's start with the most obvious level of compositional stealing: quoting from other composers' works, or transplanting whole ideas from the musical world out there into your own composition. There are different levels of this process, from entire genres that are made from sampling, such as the Canadian composer John Oswald's plunderphonics – the radical aesthetic made in the 1990s from a music that uses only samples of pre-existing sounds – or the American composer John Zorn's cut-up pieces that draw on fragments of repertoire from Bartók to Stockhausen to Ives, to produce extravagant sonic collages. And there's the electronic sampling of riffs, stems and beats that's the stock-in-trade of hip hop, steeped in homages and dialogues with the work of other artists, so each track and each album makes a palimpsest of new and overlaid meanings as each sample is used and reused. In hip hop, new contexts are created by using the same patterns and ideas in new ways, with new commentaries and combinations.

> The fetish of originality is an original sin of the classical music canon that masks a much messier and more uncomfortable truth.

And those strategies are also crucial to the music we call classical. It's not only Igor Stravinsky, so much of whose musical life proves his own maxim that 'good composers borrow, great composers steal' – above all in his ballet *Pulcinella*, a piece of utterly original, yet utterly purloined, pastiche (*see pages 56–60*). Dmitry Shostakovich 'steals', outrageously and surreally, from Gioachino Rossini in the first movement of his 15th Symphony. The way that Shostakovich works with an incipit of Rossini's *William Tell* overture – exactly *The Lone Ranger* rhythm and melody, for those who remember the way it's used in that TV theme tune – proves just how creatively catalysing these quotations can be when they're used in a symphonic context. Rossini's tune is an alien interloper when we first hear it; it's as if the skin of the

Borrowers Aloft: whether it was Mozart pilfering from Handel *(top)*, J. S. Bach remodelling Vivaldi *(bottom)* or Shostakovich raiding Rossini *(top opposite)*, composers have begged, borrowed and stolen across the centuries

symphony were punctured by music from another world of memory and reference. Shostakovich is using this quotation to play with our expectations as listeners: Rossini suddenly appears in the context of a first movement that presents surfaces that sound chirrupy and toy-like, but that are progressively revealed as weird bits of a musical jigsaw, shapes that become ever more chaotic and unpredictable.

Shostakovich compared this movement of the 15th Symphony to a toyshop; but, if it is, this is a shop of musical objects that spiral out of control, in which automata are drastically out of kilter: an emporium of warped mechanisms and disturbed and disturbing music-boxes. (Mind you, the idea of a toyshop being a site of precarious emotional and existential ambiguity is hard-wired into the Soviet psyche: the USSR's largest toyshop was in Moscow, opposite the KGB's headquarters and prison, the Lubyanka.)

The Rossini quotation stands for the surrealism of the whole movement, and the whole symphony, since the rest of the piece quotes Wagner and Rachmaninov, as well as Shostakovich's own symphonic back catalogue, over its three subsequent movements. The whole piece bears witness to the ridiculousness of the search for originality or for an original voice: instead of a reliable, single compositional presence, this symphony creates a multiple, zombie authorship, both Shostakovich's own and not his own.

Quotations always open up the potential for interpretation, but they need not be

as cryptic as they are in Shostakovich's 15th. Take the case of the Dresden Amen, a religious chord sequence for sung 'Amens', originally composed in the 18th century by Johann Gottlieb Neumann for the Royal Chapel in Dresden – and quoted in many pieces of orchestral and choral music ever since, most famously by Mendelssohn and Wagner. In Mendelssohn's 'Reformation' Symphony (No. 5), the Dresden Amen is used as a symbol of the symphony's trajectory of dramatising Protestant spiritual victory: Mendelssohn used this familiar sonic icon as a way of communicating to audiences who would have recognised the theme and its associations, making a legible interpolation into the programmatic fabric of his symphony.

In Wagner's final opera, Parsifal, the Dresden Amen is a sounding symbol of the fellowship of the Grail. Wagner's use of this theme is more radical, because he wants this tune's religiosity to become Parsifal's own, not the musical property of the Protestant Church. In the way that Wagner's music transforms this melody, and in how he uses it as one of the hallucinogenic musical spells that conjure the world of the Grail, the Dresden Amen is folded into the experience of Parsifal's redemption. By the end of the opera, you feel that the Dresden Amen belongs to Wagner's Parsifal, not to the Church: Wagner literally wants his music to become its own world, to be more meaningful than the religious traditions for which

Borrowings Avenged: Ed Sheeran and Pharrell Williams are among the many artists and bands who have fallen foul of the courts for alleged copyright infringement

this musical formula was originally composed. This is quotation as hubris: Wagner flaunts the un-originality of his idea of stealing the Dresden Amen from the Church, and from Mendelssohn, and turns its meaning inside out.

Those are just a couple of examples of how *not* having an original idea is, in fact, one of the most uniquely enriching things that you can do as a composer. The more familiar the quotes and ideas you steal, the more you can play with your audience's expectations – the more you can invite us in as listeners, and invite us to interpret what we're hearing.

In fact, at a broader level, quotation, reference and allusion act as creative commons across listenership and composition. The way composers use them allows us to understand the nature of the novelty of what a composer or a performance is really up to. That's what happens, for example, in the use of the popular tune 'L'homme armé' as musical material in so many Masses of the 15th and 16th centuries, from composers including Josquin des Prez, who wrote two Masses on this tune and whose quincentenary is celebrated at this year's Proms (*see pages 82–83*). It continues in the repertoire of so-called 'parody Masses' of the 16th century, which are all about reusing other composers' work in new contexts. And it's what the Baroque fascination for familiar bass lines and tunes is all about, as with the sorrowing descent of Dido's lament in Purcell's *Dido and Aeneas*, which has chromatic cousins and close relatives in countless chaconnes,

Going for a Song?

OLUFUNMILAYO AREWA looks into how copyright law protects but also commodifies artists and their work

In the time of J. S. Bach and Handel, composers were free to copy music by their colleagues into their own works. Culturally and legally – there was no concept of creative ownership.

Soon afterwards (1777 in the UK and 1831 in the USA) copyright laws – previously introduced to protect literary works – were extended to cover sheet music. For the first time, composers had ownership rights in their works and could enjoy income from sheet music sales.

The rising power of composers led to disputes with performers, for instance, in the case of 'insertion arias' (arias inserted into operas, mainly by singers, to best show off their individual abilities). Audiences apparently loved them. Composers did not, including Verdi, who put clauses in his contracts to prevent such changes. By the end of the 19th century, copyright-owners had the right to be compensated for public performances, which added to their income streams.

Alongside the benefits to creators, the law has enabled commercial interests, such as the record and publishing industries, to profit from the creative efforts of others. Recorded music involves two copyrights, one for the composition, the other for the sound recording. The recording industry earns the lion's share of proceeds from recorded music,

today primarily from streaming, leading to widespread complaints about both compensation and control, even from highly successful artists. Taylor Swift is re-recording her early music in an attempt to capture sales and licensing revenue from songs whose master recordings are owned by her former record label.

Copyright in the music business unfolds to a significant degree in the shadow of industry contracts. Many recording artists have signed standard-form (also known as 'take-it-or-leave-it') contracts that they believe unfairly exploit them. Most successful artists earn more from performing than from their record contracts. Even songwriters have now seen their revenue streams further subdivided. The average *Billboard* Hot 100 song credited two songwriters in 1990 but by 2020 this had grown to more than five songwriters, partly owing to contributors other than songwriters taking a share of songwriting credits (and royalties).

The question has been raised as to whether copyright laws protect artists. Copyright has granted ownership rights to creators but has led to continuing struggles over what those rights actually mean, not least in terms of borrowing, or sampling – a practice widespread in hip hop and electronic music, and one that Bach and Handel were free to enjoy.

Olufunmilayo Arewa is Murray H. Shusterman Professor of Transactional and Business Law at Temple University, Philadelphia.

chaconies and *ciaccone*. Without all of this compositional commonality – unoriginality – it would be impossible for performers, congregations and audiences to measure just how creative were the new contexts that all of these composers were catalysing from these familiar elements of musical culture.

Playing with expectations, leading our listening on journeys from familiarity to unfamiliarity: that's what every jazz musician does in any improvisation on the standards, and it's what every performer at this year's Proms season will be doing with the music they're playing. We couldn't know how creative the conductor Teodor Currentzis or violinist Patricia Kopatchinskaja are being when they play Beethoven or Tchaikovsky if they weren't playing music – quoting music – that was potentially so familiar in their concerts. Classical music works as a culture of endless cover versions in which it's precisely the unoriginality of the repertoire that allows differences between performers and performances to be felt so keenly.

That's even true for the new pieces that will be premiered this Proms season, which will all be measured and felt against the music we have all previously experienced. That's the only way that any new piece can ever be legible: if there were no possibility of a piece sparking off connections in our synapses with resonances in the rest of our musical lives, it would be condemned to monad-like muteness, incapable of communicative connection. And that never happens, even when composers have solemnly strived to create originality for originality's sake, whether they're Schubert or Stockhausen or Kaija Saariaho. Which shows that the Venn diagrams of musical and human connection are always in play when we listen to music, whether that's through quotation and reference, or the way composers manipulate and subvert our expectations across whole genres, forms and structures.

Originality is an illusion. If it exists at all, it's only through the way that pre-existing sounds and ideas are combined. The newness is in the context, in the present tense of composition or performance.

And that's not a problem – or at least it's only a problem for the originality fetishists and the canonisers of classical music. Instead of chasing that illusory originality, why don't we instead celebrate the connections? There's no problem with those commonalities of tune or structure, bass line or harmonisation that we experience when we listen to the music we love the most. Because musical works are as similar – and as varied – as what we look like as human beings. It's only through acknowledging what we share that we can understand the differences between us. And that's how composition and performance also work, as a series of family resemblances, resonating endlessly with one another across time, as individual yet as familiar as our faces are to each other. What an unoriginal thought …!●

Tom Service presents *The Listening Service*, *Music Matters* and other programmes for BBC Radio 3 and has also presented Proms and music documentaries on BBC TV. A writer for *The Guardian* since 1999, he is also the author of *Music as Alchemy* and *Thomas Adès: Full of Noises*.

❝ If copyright law had been around in 18th-century Germany and Austria, Johann Sebastian Bach, George Frideric Handel, Wolfgang Amadeus Mozart – and all the rest – would have been found guilty of plagiarism, pilfery, passing other composers' work off as their own and engaging in acts of copyright-infringing delinquency. ❞

History made with love

28 August - 26 September 2021

GEORGE ENESCU FESTIVAL

25th Jubilee Edition

FOR THE EXPRESSIVE

For the forward thinkers, makers, debaters and creators.
The pioneers who ask why. And why not.
For tomorrow's leaders;
not defined by where they have gone.
But where they are yet to go.

www.uppingham.co.uk

UPPINGHAM

1584 Forward

Lancing College

Senior School & Sixth Form

Be inspired
Be brilliant
Be you

Music Scholarships and Exhibitions available

**YOUR
INCREDIBLE
JOURNEY**

An Indomitable Maverick

From child-prodigy pianist and orchestral player to conductor and composer, Ruth Gipps enjoyed a career that was as long as it was varied. JILL HALSTEAD reflects on the woman whose clear-sighted determination and boundless energy made a lasting impression on post-war Britain's musical life

n 22 August 1942, a 21-year-old Ruth Gipps made her Proms debut when her tone-poem *Knight in Armour* was premiered on the Last Night by the BBC Symphony Orchestra under Henry Wood. A precocious musical talent, she had given her debut recital in London playing the piano aged 4. Her first compositions were published by Forsyth Brothers when she was 8 and by the age of 10 she was performing concertos with local orchestras.

Gipps was born on 20 February 1921 in Bexhill-on-Sea to an English father and Swiss mother. Her parents were both trained musicians and the family home doubled as the Bexhill School of Music. Music was a way of life for Gipps and, unlike many child prodigies, her early promise led to a career that continued long past her youth. She produced well over 100 works, including five symphonies, six concertos, numerous tone-poems, four string quartets and many large-scale choral works.

Gipps received her musical training from her mother, the formidable Hélène Gipps, who closely guarded every aspect of her daughter's education until Ruth gained a place at London's Royal College of Music in 1937. Here she studied piano with Arthur Alexander and Kendall Taylor, oboe with Leon Goossens and composition with Gordon Jacob, R. O. Morris and Ralph Vaughan Williams. Her time with Vaughan Williams would shape the course of her future work and bestowed a lifelong reverence for the man and his music.

Gipps began to establish herself as a composer during the upheaval of the war years. She had a tremendous energy for music-making, often taking on multiple roles in the same event. Her ambitions were amply demonstrated at one concert in March 1945, at which time she was working as an oboist with what was then called the City of Birmingham Orchestra. She played in Rimsky-Korsakov's *Capriccio espagnol*, then appeared as soloist in Glazunov's Piano Concerto in F minor, returning after the interval to play oboe again in her own Symphony No. 1. Such events were thrilling for Gipps, but her mix of ambition and awkwardness made her unpopular with colleagues, and ultimately led to her removal from the orchestra a year later.

Undaunted, she pursued new outlets for performance. In the early 1950s she began to train as a conductor – 'to a chorus of disapproval', as she put it. Discrimination was quite open, and she was often told that women were not capable of leading orchestras. She even struggled to find suitable tuition. Of this time she later noted: 'I didn't think of turning into a professional conductor; for a woman, conducting was unthinkable, almost indecent.' Typically, she persisted in the face of such opposition, eventually taking lessons with Stanford Robinson and gaining a position as Chorus Director of the City of Birmingham Choir and later as Conductor of the Birmingham Co-Operative Amateur Orchestra. By 1957 she had debuted at the Royal Festival Hall, conducting the Pro Arte Orchestra and the Goldsmiths Choral Union in a programme that featured Beethoven's 'Choral' Symphony. Reviewers marvelled, one noting that witnessing a woman conducting such a work was about as unlikely as a woman 'piloting a space rocket'. By the end of her career she had conducted many of the major British orchestras, including the London Symphony, London Philharmonic and most of the BBC orchestras.

Her efforts did much to improve professional opportunities for other women. She defied the conventions of the era by continuing to work after marrying in 1942, completing her DMus degree at Durham University (while seven months pregnant) to become one of the youngest Doctors of Music at the time. As a member of the Society of Women Musicians she also campaigned to end the practice of excluding married women from orchestras, something that remained widespread well into the 1960s.

Yet some of her most significant achievements came through the opportunities she carved out for herself running her own orchestras. In 1954 she founded the One Rehearsal Orchestra, subsequently known as the London Repertoire Orchestra. Gipps specifically conceived the LRO to provide experience for young musicians in performing new

▲ Gipps rehearsing at London's Royal Festival Hall where, in February 1957, she made her professional conducting debut

Yet, as the 1950s brought forward a range of modernist approaches, Gipps's musical style was increasingly seen as outdated. Her private disdain quickly turned to public confrontation, with statements branding avant-garde music as 'utter rubbish' and 'a deliberate conning of the public'. There were published exchanges with composers such as Reginald Smith Brindle, whose work she dismissed as 'nonsense.' Gipps's attacks broadened into long-running disputes with institutions such as the BBC, consolidating her reputation as a maverick.

Gipps dedicated her life to music-making and her contribution to post-war musical life in Britain was significant. In a 1975 interview she reflected: 'I have put music before everything else all my life, showing a scale of values that perhaps … is lacking in humanity, but that is inevitable and right for me.' Her devotion was absolute and did not make her an 'easy person', as she was quick to admit. Yet it was precisely this determined belief in herself as a composer and performer that proved essential to her breaking down barriers that had traditionally silenced women's contributions to musical life. ●

Jill Halstead is a Professor of Music at the Grieg Academy, University of Bergen. Her work focuses on questions of gender and music and includes the books *The Woman Composer: Creativity and the Gendered Politics of Musical Composition* and *Ruth Gipps: Anti-Modernism, Nationalism and Difference in English Music*.

Symphony No. 2
5 AUGUST

Sea-Shore Suite
30 AUGUST

repertoire with limited rehearsal time – in line with professional practice. During the 31 years she ran the LRO, hundreds of musicians passed through on their way to becoming professional players. In 1961 she founded the professional Chanticleer Orchestra, which she ran alongside the LRO for 20 years. It would contribute much to the independent concert scene of 1960s and 1970s London, particularly through Gipps's championing of lesser-known British composers, including herself.

Indeed, her trailblazing conducting work became a crucial factor in her continued development as a composer. Historically women have had few opportunities to write large-scale orchestral works, but through the formation of her own orchestras Gipps created a crucial platform which allowed her to develop and flourish as an orchestral composer through her middle and later years.

Her orchestral works were among her best, with the last three symphonies – completed between 1965 and 1982 – exemplifying her particular brand of memorable melody and luscious, shifting harmony. She defined her music as 'obviously and incurably English': a continuation of the legacy of Arthur Bliss, William Walton and Vaughan Williams. Committed to the national Romanticism which flourished in the early part of the century, her work often drew on evocative, rural- and nature-inspired themes, which remained popular with concert audiences in the post-war years.

Gipps consults the score of her Fourth Symphony (1972) with friend and fellow composer Arthur Bliss, an advocate of her music to whom she dedicated the work

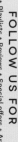

Past Progressive

In his ballet *Pulcinella* Stravinsky reimagined the cool Classical lines of the music of Pergolesi and others from his unique, 20th-century perspective. This fascination with existing types, says STEPHEN WALSH, raised the curtain on an array of stylistic 'borrowings' that inspired the ever-curious composer to reinvent himself for the future

One of the best known of Igor Stravinsky's many gnomic utterances about his own music was made about his ballet Pulcinella. 'Pulcinella,' he told his assistant Robert Craft, 'was my discovery of the past, the epiphany through which the whole of my late work became possible.' Like a lot of things in the Stravinsky-Craft conversation books, it's a remark that needs treating with care. Of course, Stravinsky knew all about the past already. After all, his father had been Principal Bass at the Marinsky Theatre in St Petersburg; the young Igor had known many of the Russian composers of his day and much of the past repertoire. A photograph survives of him in his room aged about 15 with a whole gallery of composer portraits on the wall behind him: Wagner, Schumann, Berlioz, Beethoven and several others.

But the epiphany image has to be understood in relation to the actual composition of Pulcinella. The suggestion came from Sergey Diaghilev, founder of the Ballets Russes, in 1919, and as much as anything it was a device to keep the composer onside, at a time when the Stravinsky ballet that really interested him was the not-yet fully completed Les noces. Pulcinella would be a set of orchestrations of unpublished pieces written by the 18th-century composer Pergolesi that Diaghilev and the dancer-choreographer Léonide Massine had dug up in the Naples Conservatory, to go with a ballet Massine was planning round the characters of the commedia dell'arte (the pieces weren't all by Pergolesi, but that's a detail). The Ballets Russes had already danced The Good-Humoured Ladies to music by Scarlatti arranged by Tommasini, and La boutique fantasque to Rossini arranged by Respighi. Pulcinella would be Pergolesi-Stravinsky, and Igor could do it in his sleep. It would be a jolly commedia show, with brilliant Cubist sets by Picasso and a dazzling cast of dancers that included Massine himself, Tamara Karsavina, Lubov Tchernicheva and Stanislas Idzikowski.

It didn't work out quite like that, at least where the music was concerned. When Stravinsky looked closely at the material, it began to intrigue him, and he started marking it up on the copyist's manuscript. In other words, he was adding notes, not just indicating orchestration. Pergolesi was being modernised; not to put too fine a point on it, it was being Stravinskyised. In the very first piece, for example (actually a movement from a trio sonata by Domenico Gallo), the simple harmonies of the original were touched up with added notes that clashed gently but naggingly with the existing ones, and at the end of the first musical paragraph figures were repeated and barrings altered so that the final phrase began to sound like a rhythmic pattern out out of Stravinsky's own earlier ballets, Petrushka or even The Rite of Spring. These compositional effects in Pulcinella are fairly discreet, but they clearly gave Stravinsky an idea, and he was soon doing something similar with material he invented himself but with conscious reference to styles distant from his own. He wrote Mavra (1921–2), a little opera aping the Russian vaudeville style of Glinka's day, and the Octet (1922–3), a sparkling piece of fake – well, what? Bach? Haydn? Beethoven? Nothing chimes at all obviously, yet the music clearly reaches out from the 20th century to the 18th or early 19th, if only by being in a key (E flat) instead of some antique mode or other, and by having first and second subjects linked by a sort of transition, as in Classical sonata form. And so Stravinskyan neo-Classicism was born.

> **Stravinsky himself once admitted that 'whatever interests me, whatever I love, I wish to make my own (I am probably describing a rare form of kleptomania)'.**

The idea wasn't entirely new, even in his own work. During the war he had composed a number of short pieces in Western idioms: a waltz, an española, a polka. In The Soldier's Tale of 1918 the princess had danced to another waltz, a tango and a ragtime; then there was a separate ensemble piece called Ragtime, and, after the war, the Piano Rag Music.

▶ A sketch for Pulcinella by Pablo Picasso, who was charged with designing the sets and costumes for its premiere in May 1920

But these were genre pieces that anyone might have written. What began with *Mavra* was something more like a modelling process. It asked the question: what would an opera by Alyabyev or Gurilyov (Russian salon composers of the 1830s) sound like if I, Igor Stravinsky, were to recompose it? What would a piano sonata by Clementi be like? How would an opera based on *Oedipus rex* work if it were patched together by different composers acting through me as a medium? If, to ask the question in a slightly different way, I were to take an imaginary symphony by Beethoven and rewrite it using the techniques I originally evolved in my Russian ballets, would it make any sense?

I'm not of course suggesting that Stravinsky asked himself these questions in these ways. The composer will surely have simply composed, following impulses from way below any surface intention. But then why did it suddenly happen in this way at that time?

After the First World War, revivalism was in the air. To carry on where the world had left off in 1914 seemed not to be an option. But to invent new ways of doing things from scratch wasn't much better as an idea, though one or two composers (notably the Futurist Luigi Russolo) tried it. The Catholic thinker Jacques Maritain called for a way out of 'the immense intellectual disarray inherited from the 19th century'; Jean Cocteau proclaimed a 'rappel à l'ordre' – a recall to order (though it must be said that his own lifestyle in the mid-1920s was hardly the ideal model). Order, in any case, meant going

back to the old ways – to a time when art was balanced and harmonious; perhaps to a time when, to quote Maritain again, art was 'honest labour', a making, not an expressing. As with all such backward projections, from Hesiod's 'Golden Age' onwards, there was a good deal of fantasising about these ideas. Writing about his Octet, Stravinsky insisted that 'this sort of music has no other aim than to be sufficient in itself. In general, I consider that music is only able to solve musical problems; and nothing else, neither the literary nor the picturesque, can be in music of any real interest. The play of musical elements is the thing.'

The expressionless gaze is often a defence mechanism of the vulnerable, and the world certainly felt vulnerable in 1918. Stravinsky, trapped in Switzerland since 1914 and now, after the 1917 revolutions, effectively barred for ever from his homeland, was a living, breathing example. The folk music and folk poetry of Russia had been the lifeblood of his music since *The Firebird: Les noces* – still a work in progress – and the *Symphonies of Wind Instruments*, compiled in 1920 out of wartime sketches, reeked of Russian soil, Russian ceremony. But now he was rapidly losing contact with those things, and it was becoming necessary to reinvent himself.

This is perhaps the chief message of *The Soldier's Tale*, about the exiled soldier who, on trying to revisit his homeland, is grabbed by the Devil and, presumably, carted off to Hell. The music is hybrid – part Russian, part foreign (Stravinsky

Movers and shakers: Pablo Picasso (*second left*) and Igor Stravinsky (*second right*), two of the creative forces behind *Pulcinella*, in 1926; the pair are flanked by Jean Cocteau and Picasso's first wife, Olga

did genuinely fear that, if he went back to Russia, he would be grabbed by the devil of Communism, which is indeed what happened to Prokofiev). So for him stylistic modelling was a necessity beyond the generally felt wish to restore order. It was a *sine qua non* of continuing to compose at all, and this is why his borrowings, to call them that, soon strayed far and wide beyond what might conceivably be called the Classical, embracing Romantic composers such as Verdi, Delibes and Tchaikovsky, as well as jazz, circus music, Hollywood and even travel-poster Russianism. It was all the same. The result was always Stravinsky.

But is it fair to describe them as borrowings? Borrowing implies repayment, which is hardly possible here. Let's call a spade a spade and talk about theft. Stravinsky himself once admitted that 'whatever interests me, whatever I love, I wish to make my own (I am probably describing a rare form of kleptomania)'. But the theft of a style is not quite the same as the kind of theft known as plagiarism (or, to use a more polite term, quotation), and Stravinsky in point of fact quotes from other music rather seldom, unless of course we count folk song, which is common property. *Petrushka* contains a copyright tune that he heard played by a hurdy-gurdy in the South of France, and assumed to be a traditional melody; had he known it was in copyright he would have avoided it, at its cost him a great deal in royalties. There is a snatch of Rossini, the overture to *The Barber of Seville*, in *Jeu de cartes*

❝ Stravinsky's serialism always retained this pitch-sensitive, if not always tonal, character, and often seems to tread a dangerous path between the preservation of his own personal method ... and a deep-seated need for prestige with the young avant-garde. ❞

But Stravinsky would have had no truck with the kind of referential quotation that turned into a virtual aesthetic movement in the 1960s and 1970s as an escape route from the arid terrain of compulsory serialism. His nearest approach to anything of the sort was his Ida Rubinstein ballet *The Fairy's Kiss* (1928), which was intended as a kind of Pulcinellification of Tchaikovsky, but eventually turned into a re-compositional

(1936) and a galumphing quotation from Schubert's D major *Marche militaire* in the *Circus Polka*, a ballet originally performed in 1942 by Barnum and Bailey's circus elephants. A fragment of the last-act quartet from Mozart's *Così fan tutte* pops up, almost by accident, in the solo horn introduction to Tom's aria 'Vary the song' in his 1951 opera *The Rake's Progress*, and one might briefly detect the F major Ballade of Chopin (a composer Stravinsky once told his son, Soulima, didn't interest him) at the start of the *Serenade in A* (1925).

Symphonies of Wind Instruments
(1920, rev. 1945, 1947)

This arose from a 1920 commission for a commemorative Debussy supplement of the French music magazine *La revue musical*. Stravinsky submitted a chorale for piano from a recent sketchbook, but then decided to enlarge it into a piece for wind instruments, adding more sketches until he had a nine-minute piece in a novel form of alternating sections ending with the original chorale. It remained unpublished until a 1947 revision, which regularised the scoring but kept the idiosyncratic, brilliantly effective form.

Symphony in C (1938–40)

A Chicago Symphony Orchestra commission, written between Beverly Hills, Massachusetts and Sancellemoz sanatorium (*above*), the *Symphony in C* is a symbolic response, a typical work for a prestigious symphony concert. It is hardly 'in C', but is built around a mixture of C major and E minor. It has the usual four movements, the usual Classical orchestra, the familiar formal outlines. Yet its procedures all come ultimately from the composer's Russian way of doing things. Typical Stravinskyan neo-Classicism: he has you thinking Classical but twists everything his way.

process so elaborate that he nearly missed the performance deadline.

As for escape routes, his own tactic was to head straight into the enemy camp and adopt his own form of serialism. It all came out of his first post-war visit to Europe (from California, where he had been living since 1941), to conduct the premiere of *The Rake's Progress* in Venice in September 1951. After the premiere he went to Germany and was introduced to recordings of music by Schoenberg and Webern and, notoriously, Boulez's *Polyphonie X*, and he realised, somewhat to his dismay, that his own recent music cut no ice with progressive young European musicians. A period of depression followed; then, returning to composition, he started picking up threads from *The Rake's Progress* and composed the *Cantata* (1951–2), using verse-and-refrain forms that had lain hidden in the design of the opera.

The *Cantata* also tries out a modest and highly un-Schoenbergian serialism in the form of an 11-note row, with several repeated notes (instead of the usual 12, all different) and a strongly tonal feel, something Schoenberg, who had considerably died the year Stravinsky began the *Cantata*, would probably have regarded as a hopeless compromise. But Stravinsky's serialism always retained this pitch-sensitive, if not always tonal, character, and often seems to tread a dangerous path between the preservation of his own personal method, based on melodic line, rhythm and the precise voicing of chords, and a deep-seated need for prestige with the young avant-garde. The fact that several of his serial works are masterpieces superior to anything by that particular set of composers may act as a warning to us never to judge a work of art by its creator's motives.

Does neo-Classicism ever rear its head in any form in these serial pieces? Perhaps remotely in *Agon* (1953–7), where dances such as the bransle and the galliard reflect the ballet's origins in a 17th-century dance manual, though even when some faint air of the past does leak out, the music's amazing originality of sound and discourse makes sure there is never any sense of pastiche. The fascinating thing about this and other Stravinsky proto-serial works of the 1950s is how they suggested to certain younger composers (I'm thinking, for instance, of Luciano Berio and Sir Harrison Birtwistle) ways of absorbing the past into an entirely modern way of thinking. And it may be that this was precisely what motivated Stravinsky himself when he first turned to other styles in order to fertilise his own. ●

Stephen Walsh is the author of a major two-volume biography of Stravinsky as well as, more recently, a study of the Russian nationalists, Musorgsky and His Circle, and a biography of Debussy. He is currently writing a short history of 19th-century music.

Pulcinella
6 AUGUST

Symphonies of Wind Instruments; Symphony in C; Symphony in Three Movements
22 AUGUST

See Index for other Stravinsky works

Symphony in Three Movements (1942–5)

The first movement (with solo piano) was composed in 1942, apparently as refreshment from hack American commissions; the second movement (with harp) in 1943, supposedly for the film *The Song of Bernadette*; the finale (piano and harp) in time for the New York premiere in January 1946. The outer movements are closer to the dionysiac Stravinsky of *The Rite of Spring* than anything since that work. At the time he denied they had a war programme, but later claimed they had.

Tres sacrae cantiones (1957–9)

These three pieces are completions of three sacred motets (published 1603) by Gesualdo (*above*), which had survived incomplete, with two of the seven part-books missing. Stravinsky composed the missing parts with his tongue not far from his cheek. Although Gesualdo often wrote daring harmonies (and, by the way, murdered his wife and her lover), Stravinsky added one or two that Gesualdo would probably not have thought of. Even so, Stravinsky's versions were included in the collected Gesualdo edition.

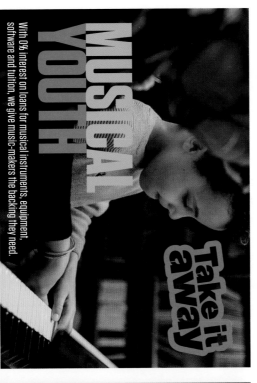

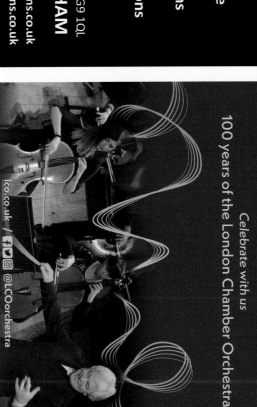

A Family Affair

As the Kanneh-Mason siblings perform their *Carnival of the Animals* project live for the first time, REBECCA FRANKS speaks to pianist Isata, the eldest, about Saint-Saëns's playful score and working with the author Michael Morpurgo

uring the first national lockdown, back in the spring of 2020, the whole Kanneh-Mason family found itself under one roof for the first time in years. 'It was like an alternate world,' recalls Isata Kanneh-Mason, the eldest of the seven siblings who were once dubbed 'Britain's most musical family'. 'In some ways it was just like going back to childhood, as suddenly we were all together in the same house, and it hadn't been that way for years.'

The five eldest – Isata (25), Braimah (23), Sheku (22), Konya (20) and Jeneba (18) – temporarily left behind their performing and student lives in London to return to the family home in Nottingham, joining the two youngest children, Aminata (15) and Mariatu (11), and their parents.

The Kanneh-Masons have always played music together. The year before cellist Sheku made headlines winning BBC Young Musician in 2016, he and five of his siblings had found fame when they reached the semi-finals of ITV's *Britain's Got Talent*. In the tough times of the pandemic, music proved a welcome outlet for the family. They let the world share it too, hosting regular Facebook Live videos from home and inviting broadcaster Alan Yentob to film a joyous remote-access documentary for the BBC TV series *imagine* …. The siblings also had the spark of an idea for a new album,

which would see them all record together for the first time. 'We grew up with a recording of Prokofiev's *Peter and the Wolf*, narrated by Dame Edna Everage. We loved it so much,' says Isata. 'The words really brought the music and instruments to life for us.'

Inspired by this blend of notes and words, the Kanneh-Masons decided to give the same treatment to another childhood classic, Camille Saint-Saëns's *The Carnival of the Animals*. They asked their record company to invite Michael Morpurgo, the former Children's Laureate whose novel *War Horse* became a hit theatre production, to collaborate with them. 'Luckily, when we approached him to ask if he would do the project, his answer was to send the poems – already written and finished!' recalls Isata. Next stop, last summer, was Abbey Road Studios in London to make the album. The resultant recording is a sheer delight. All seven siblings perform, on either violin, cello or piano, and are joined by a handful of guest musicians, while Morpurgo shares poetry-reading duty with actress Olivia Colman. His words are witty and warm, an ideal companion to Saint-Saëns's music. The album was released last autumn, and this year the Kanneh-Masons will be heading to the BBC Proms to perform their *Carnival* project live for the first time. They'll be joined onstage by Morpurgo, as well as the other instrumentalists from the recording, including violist Timothy Ridout, violinist Ayla Sahin and clarinettist Mark Simpson. 'It's very

exciting,' says Isata. 'We're all really looking forward to it.'

Saint-Saëns composed his 'grand zoological fantasy' in early 1886, when he was on holiday in Austria. The 50-year-old composer was supposed to be busy writing his 'Organ' Symphony (No. 3), commissioned by Britain's Royal Philharmonic Society, but instead he found his attention diverted elsewhere. What started off as just 'The Swan' – a solo for the renowned cellist Charles Lebouc – soon blossomed into 14 movements depicting the characters, charms and foibles of an assortment of animals. Though the piece was not as serious as the symphony he had begun writing, Saint-Saëns gleefully wrote to his publisher: 'But it's such fun!'

> " Saint-Saëns paints his miniature portraits with evocative instrumental colours: the xylophone suggests ancient bones in 'Fossils'; the pianos ripple like silky water in 'Aquarium'. He also packs the piece with all sorts of musical references … "

The music poured out, and within days *The Carnival of the Animals* was finished. The piece sparkles with joy and wit, and, as Isata notes, the writing is wonderfully visual. Painting was, after all, part of the

▲ The seven Kanneh-Mason siblings, depicted alongside some of the characters from Saint-Saëns's 'grand zoological fantasy'.

polymath Saint-Saëns's long list of interests and accomplishments, which ranged from astronomy and botany to philosophy and travel. In *The Carnival of the Animals*, he paints his miniature portraits with evocative instrumental colours: the xylophone suggests ancient bones in 'Fossils'; the pianos ripple like silky water in 'Aquarium'.

He also packs the piece with all sorts of musical references, an extra layer of fun for those who would like to spot them. One example is the way he slows down the upbeat cancan – the tune is the 'infernal galop' from Offenbach's operetta *Orpheus in the Underworld* – to depict the lethargic tortoises. Elsewhere the 'Elephant' – a growly double bass – dances to music borrowed from Mendelssohn's ethereal *A Midsummer Night's Dream* and the featherlight 'Dance of the Sylphs' from Berlioz's *The Damnation of Faust* – 54 years before Walt Disney showcased a hippopotamus pirouetting to Ponchielli's 'Dance of the Hours' in his 1940 film *Fantasia*.

'My favourite moment is the duet between Braimah and Ayla when they play "Characters with Long Ears"', laughs Isata. 'It's such a quirky movement, and it's amazing how much texture you can have from two violin players.' And did Saint-Saëns add in a little extra amusement for himself in this onomatopoeic sketch, suggesting those braying donkeys could be music critics? They certainly wouldn't be the only humans in the menagerie: the 'Pianists' are later held captive by endless

scales – surely familiar territory for Saint-Saëns, whose piano gifts were such that by the age of 10 he could play all 32 of Beethoven's piano sonatas from memory.

Saint-Saëns was himself one of the pianists at the first outing of *The Carnival of the Animals*, which took place in private on 3 March 1886. The piece was performed a few more times at private events, often with musicians wearing animal masks, while one occasion 'ended up in roars of laughter'. Yet Saint-Saëns would only allow 'The Swan' – reassuringly elegant and beautiful – to be published in his lifetime, for fear all this frivolity would damage his reputation as a serious composer. Accordingly, it wasn't until 1922, the year after his death, that the whole suite was first published.

Contrary to the composer's anxieties, a serious approach is actually needed for this piece, suggests Isata. Kanneh-Mason rehearsals are, she says, focused and respectful: 'Everyone immediately switches into professional mode.' While preparing for this project, they read Morpurgo's poetry out loud to help bring the music to life, and focused on finding as much detail in the music as they could. Of course, Saint-Saëns wasn't entirely wrong. Once the hard work of rehearsing was done, says Isata, 'we let all of that go and had fun with it'. ●

Rebecca Franks is a classical music critic for *The Times*, and works as an arts journalist, writer and editor.

Saint-Saëns The Carnival of the Animals
29 AUGUST

See Index for other Saint-Saëns works

Animal Magic

Michael Morpurgo on reimagining Saint-Saëns's musical menagerie

Sometimes for me the best inspiration is simply to be asked to do the extraordinary. One day the summer before last, a producer at Decca asked if I would like to write poems for a new disc the Kanneh-Mason family wanted to make of *The Carnival of the Animals*. I knew Ogden Nash had done this a while back, so I was as pleased as I was surprised to be asked.

Since I first listened to *Peter and the Wolf* as a child I have loved the weaving together of words and music. More recently, I have loved giving story concerts alongside musicians. But this was different. I was being asked to recreate, in my own voice, a great classic of orchestral music for children. And I was to perform alongside the most extraordinary family of young musicians I had ever heard.

I wrote the 14 poems on holiday in Greece, on Ithaca, in just a few days. Some say that Homer wrote *The Odyssey* there, by the side of the same 'wine-dark sea'. Remarkably, the Kanneh-Mason family liked them. I was told that Olivia Colman, no less, was going to share the readings with me. My cup was running over.

Then, during the pandemic, my wife and I made a trip to London to record *Carnival* with the Kanneh-Masons. That was a day to remember. They played with such intensity, such sensitivity, endlessly supportive of each other. The older I get, the more inspired I am by the genius and energy of youth. And now we're to do it again at the Proms. Oh, lucky man!

THE OLD MASTERS IN NEW HANDS

Sheku Kanneh-Mason MBE plays a cello by Antonius & Hieronymus Amati, Cremona 1610 with a bow by Nicolas Maire c1855 made possible by the Florian Leonhard Fellowship

"World authority on fine violins"
FINANCIAL TIMES

"World-renowned violin dealer"
BBC Music Magazine

"The world's leading expert"
The Daily Telegraph

FLORIAN LEONHARD
FINE VIOLINS

LONDON | HONG KONG
SAN FRANCISCO | NEW YORK

violins@florianleonhard.com
www.florianleonhard.com

Tomorrow's Voices

Last year the Proms's annual composing competition, BBC Young Composer, was revamped, shifting its focus towards greater accessibility and long-term development. One of the judges, **KATE WHITLEY**, hears from some of those who took part, and reflects on how the pandemic has affected their creativity

The 2020 BBC Young Composer competition received a record-breaking number of entries: 630 young musicians submitted pieces, well over double the number of previous years. The range of music submitted was also greater, with the criteria of the competition being widened to encourage all genres, instruments and methods of music-making for the first time.

I was asked to be a judge and, while I am hesitant about the idea of music being a 'competition', last year there was a shift in focus away from the competitive element towards talent development: winners now receive additional mentoring, as well as a commission to write a new piece for the BBC Concert Orchestra. I felt really lucky, in a year that has seen so much adversity, to be part of something that highlights and celebrates the creativity and positivity of young people.

What struck me when listening to the entries, and when interviewing young composers for this article, was how composing while isolated in lockdown could be a valuable way of looking inwards – of protecting yourself from the chaos of the outside world. It was also heartening to see such a wide range of music – and great that the broadening of the competition criteria acknowledges the value of diverse musical styles and genres. I loved hearing from young composers with open minds about what musical composition is and can be.

One of those composers was 15-year-old Zac Pile, whose beautiful piece *Voice* really grabbed me in the way it combines raw, natural vocals with electronic music production. It's a very personal piece, written about Zac's experience of his voice breaking: how he could feel it getting lower but couldn't do anything to control it. 'It can be a struggle going through that,' he told me. Writing *Voice* was a way of confronting that struggle – to 'celebrate the voice as an instrument and to help me feel confident in my own voice again'.

Like Zac, 16-year-old Rowena Jones turned to writing for her own instrument when music-making with others became impossible. She played all four parts of her multi-track recorder piece *Spring2020* herself, recording them in her bedroom on her mobile phone before layering them together. Rowena had actually stopped composing last year in order to focus on her GCSEs. Then the pandemic hit, giving her a lot more time. This, she says, has allowed her to enjoy composing much more (a feeling I recognise too, and one of the pandemic's few silver linings).

Nineteen-year-old Greg May – whose piece *Toye* was a winner in the Senior category of last year's competition – spent one term at university this year before going back home to face the rest of the academic year online. He has been writing solo pieces for friends to play at home during lockdown. Writing music that is focused on a single instrument – and, again, having more time to do so – has been a really enjoyable experience for him.

66 In light of how much they were all up for trying new things, I think one of the big strengths of the recent changes to BBC Young Composer is how it's become more about nurturing young musicians, rather than rewarding existing talent. 99

While speaking to these young composers, I was also impressed by how willing they were to challenge themselves. Zac, for example, found that lockdown encouraged him to use music technology more as part of his compositional process: 'My immediate thought was, "I'm going to do this on the laptop", so I started to develop my skills and challenge myself in totally different ways.'

Greg's piece was written for an orchestra of amateur musicians, which presents a unique set of challenges, such as writing for players of a specific ability. He plays in the same orchestra so 'really knows how it ticks' but learnt a lot from navigating the practical considerations of writing for amateur musicians.

▲ The 2019 competition winners: (from top) Tom Hughes, Madeleine Chassar-Hesketh, Jacy de Sousa, Daniel Liu, Sasha Scott, Isabel Wood

In light of how much they were all up for being challenged and trying new things, I think one of the big strengths of the recent changes to BBC Young Composer is how it's become more about nurturing young musicians, rather than rewarding existing talent. This gives the competition the potential to have more impact in broadening access to music and giving opportunities to young people who wouldn't otherwise have them. The other judges and I talked a lot about this while looking through last year's entries – questioning what the role of a 'competition' should be and how it could help develop young composers while countering the biases and inequalities in our society.

It's great to see BBC Young Composer moving in this direction. When I entered, back in 2007, the prize was having your winning piece performed in a concert. Though a fantastic opportunity, this didn't have the same focus on long-term development that the new programme offers. This year, the 2020 winners will work with a composer mentor – either Dobrinka Tabakova or Gavin Higgins – on a new commission for the BBC Concert Orchestra, culminating in a broadcast performance.

Furthermore, a recent series of online workshops run by BBC Young Composer, called Composing the World Around You, responded directly to the themes that emerged in the 2020 entries, namely writing in isolation and using what's around you to create music. The series, which was open to anyone who wanted to join, also addressed the more

fundamental aspects of composing: getting started with a piece, finding your sound and dealing with writer's block and self-doubt.

The young composers I spoke to were really excited to get started on their commissions. Rowena said she is 'looking forward to listening to and learning from someone else's opinion on things', while Greg wants to 'try out ideas, develop skills and learn how to communicate with musicians I don't already know'. He also said the development programme offers the 'rare luxury of having the time to try stuff in a safe space. Knowing I can write what I want is really liberating.'

That 'safe space' idea is key – having somewhere you can try things, make mistakes and learn from them. I'm really excited that the competition is focusing on making music open to more people and on shifting perceptions of composition. It has been really heart-warming to talk to such positive, resilient and self-aware young people, who all have such an open-minded approach to music. It certainly bodes well for the future! ●

Kate Whitley is a composer and pianist. She runs the Multi-Story Orchestra, which performs in car parks around the UK. Her choral piece I am I say was performed at the Proms in 2017.

BBC Young Composer 2021

The deadline for entries to this year's competition is Monday 28 June. Entries should be submitted online, no later than 5pm. For full details of how to enter, visit bbc.co.uk/youngcomposer. The winners will be announced on the BBC Proms website by Tuesday 21 September.

Zac Pile, whose electronically produced Voice was a winner in the Lower Junior category of last year's competition

Rowena Jones, a winner in the Upper Junior category with her multi-track recorder piece Spring2020

Greg May, whose piece for amateur orchestra, Toye, was a winner in last year's Senior category

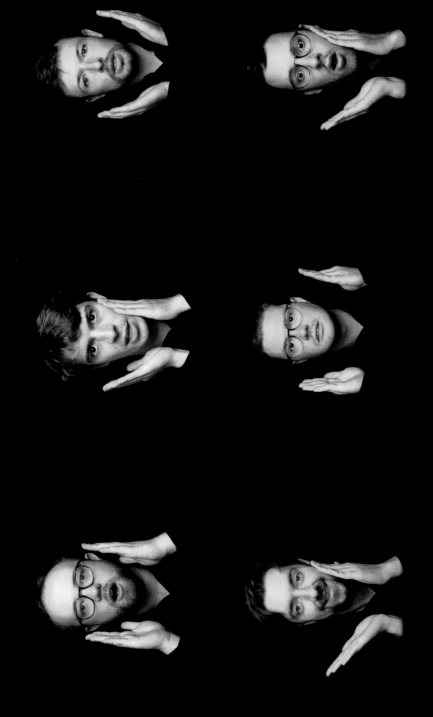

Six Degrees of Separation

What happens when the primal bond that connects performers and audiences is torn apart?
We all yearn to share the same space again but in the meantime,
says social psychologist **ALEKS KROTOSKI**, disruption has led to innovation

t's 7.30pm and Héloïse Werner is onstage at London's Wigmore Hall with her ensemble, The Hermes Experiment. As well as singing, the French soprano and composer makes non-verbal sounds and uses her body and face as percussion. 'I really love hearing people's responses,' she says, 'whether it's laughter or complete silence.'

Today, though, she is performing to an empty house. There are no friends in the front row to make eye contact with, no murmur of the crowd. Just row upon row of reminders that these are not normal times.

'It's a really funny thing, not having an audience,' Werner reflects when we speak on Zoom a month later. 'There's no walking on stage or getting into the flow. There's no human interaction, which normally really puts you into the right mindset.' The absence of physically present listeners during lockdown inspired many to reflect on the magical, alchemical spark that exists when an audience and performer share a one-of-a-kind moment in time. 'With every single listener, the thing you create changes,' explains Dalia Stasevska, the BBC Symphony Orchestra's Principal Guest Conductor. 'I change also.' The players Stasevska performs with, the audience they perform to, are 'never,

never the same' And, as we have learnt – because we spent so much time over the past year trying and failing – this cannot be digitised. Well, not yet.

There has been a lot of physiological and psychological research on what happens to individuals when they come together to form a crowd. Physiologically, their heartbeats begin to synchronise; neurologically, their brainwaves begin to mirror one another; and psychologically, they become 'deindividuated' – literally separated from a sense of individuality. All of these outcomes can feel rapturous and significant. Once an audience is in synergy, it takes its cues from the aggregate, laughing louder, applauding longer and able to turn venomous in half a beat.

Performers, too, experience this rapture. A study published in Nature Scientific Reports in May 2020 described how a group of drummers found their performances and their neurological rhythms spontaneously consolidating as they played together. Another study published the same month in the journal NeuroImage found that these rhythms can be communicated from performer to audience even when the performance is recorded. As the brainwaves align, the audience's appreciation of the music increases. But we don't know as much about the effect the audience has on the performer.

Dr Michael Christian Leitner is a psychologist in the Centre for Cognitive Neuroscience at the University of Salzburg, and a big football fan. His team,

FC Red Bull Salzburg, is a powerhouse in the Austrian league. In March last year the pandemic closed the stadium doors and threatened to cancel the season, but in June the league was allowed to resume – on the basis that no supporters would be present. Sensing an opportunity, Leitner and his colleagues decided to investigate what effect the crowd has on players' behaviour and performance.

They anticipated that players would have trouble performing as well as usual during 'ghost' games because there would be no pressure from the crowd. 'You act differently when you dance in front of a hundred people,' Leitner explained. And, indeed, players did 'dance' differently. But not in the way they expected.

Red Bull Salzburg won the Austrian Bundesliga, as they had the previous six years, so their performance as athletes didn't diminish. But, across the season, play was more civilised: there were fewer fouls for unfair sportsmanship in the ghost games, fewer physical fights and fewer altercations with referees. Leitner believes this is because the audience wasn't egging them on. 'When the crowd is screaming, it feels like they're supporting you,' he explains. 'You feel like you can let your emotions overflow.' But, when there's no crowd, you are reindividuated and you become conscious again of what it is you are doing.

Without the audience motivating them, these elite performers had to find the strength inside themselves

▲ Face time: The Gesualdo Six's online video of coronsolfège for 6, a piece the vocal group commissioned from soprano Héloïse Werner after seeing her novel lockdown Twitter performances

For listeners who have never played an instrument, this is an aspect that can easily be taken for granted. The best musicians can often make a difficult passage appear very easy or a highly stressful environment seem calm. 'It was an emotionally charged performance,' explains Ashwell, 'because, as I was playing, I was thinking, "12 people out there are holding my heartbeat. This is intense." That imagining then changed how he played, creating even more intensity, which ultimately was being fed back to the audience.

Perhaps, then, these kinds of haptic technologies could be fitted in reverse, giving the performer the physical sensation of what an audience member is feeling, thus closing that feedback loop. 'That would give us a sense of whether we were doing our job properly. And that's no bad thing,' says Ashwell. But it is both expensive and potentially distracting; instead, performers are able to use existing communication channels, such as social media, to simulate a kind of call-and-response interaction.

Héloïse Werner was in the first week of the first lockdown when she invented coronasolfège. 'I don't own a microphone, I don't know how to use any kind of software. I just have an iPhone and a music stand,' she explains. While playing around in boredom, she invented a system of non-verbal sounds using, as well as her voice, different parts of her face – biting together her teeth, slapping her cheeks, opening and closing her eyes, all in different rhythms. She recorded

to push through moments of doubt and exhaustion.

Some streaming systems have tried to mimic a crowd with live chat rooms during live concerts. But these don't benefit the performer, argues Héloïse Werner. 'It's quite nice for the audience to feel they're part of a community watching the same thing,' she says, 'but as a performer you can't monitor that. You're too busy.' Besides, she believes the feedback loop comes from the audience just being in the room. A crowd doesn't need to be chanting or yelling to make its presence felt: non-verbal communication – the shuffling of the programmes, the coughing, the breathing – tells her whether she's making a connection.

Some performers have played with haptic (ie touch) technologies, such as the vibration function on your mobile phone, to try to create a connection. At the 2015 Bristol Proms, the Sacconi Quartet put their heartbeats into the hands of the audience, using heart-rate monitors connected to vibrating handheld devices to simulate the inner experience of the musician onstage.

'We chose Beethoven's Op. 132,' explains viola player Robin Ashwell. 'It has that fantastic middle movement about life and death and emotion and hard feelings. It seemed absolutely appropriate. We wanted audience members to think about what was going on in the performers' bodies and minds and hearts when they're going through this.'

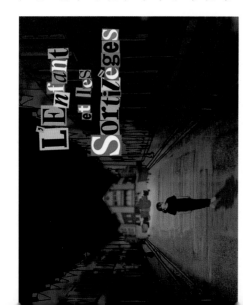

A still from Ravel's opera *L'enfant et les sortilèges* by VOPERA, the Virtual Opera Project, filmed in lockdown and digitally drawing together a cast of 80 as well as the London Philharmonic Orchestra

Playing to the cloud: pianist Stephen Hough performs to an empty house in June 2020 for one of the Wigmore Hall's many live-streamed concerts

herself in a short video, posted onto Twitter and it went viral. 'Lots of people seemed to like it,' she says. She started talking with people around the world about what she was doing, receiving requests, making suggestions. 'It was a kind of delayed audience,' she laughs. It inspired a second video. But this time was different.

'I then had the pressure of creating something even more impressive than the first one,' she says. She practised a bit, brushed her hair and put make-up on before recording. 'I thought about the audience reaction.' Across the 37 short videos (around 35–40 seconds each), Werner produced a coronasolfege catalogue and evolved from casual video-poster to audience-aware creator. Eventually, she shifted into being a performer who is confident in her work, yet conscious there are people watching. This social media-mediated experience delivered the immediate feedback she craved in her streaming performances.

Yet nothing can, or should, replace the live event – not online content or video projections or even mechanical heartbeats. The alchemy of the audience and performer coming together elevates the room, the whole performance, and reminds us, as we lose ourselves in the moment, of what it means to be alive. 'These are the moments that you remember,' says Werner. 'They are the reasons we do what we do.' ●

Aleks Krotoski is a social psychologist and broadcaster who specialises in technology and interactivity. She writes and presents Radio 4's series The Digital Human.

The Thrill of the Crowd

Violinist Tasmin Little on the 'essential ingredient' of a performance

As a young child, I remember going to social gatherings with my family and hoping desperately that someone would ask me to play my violin. Even at that tender age, it was the connection to others that drew me to performing. It wasn't just about 'showing off' (although being admired for doing something difficult and unusual was part of the appeal). It was a sense of wonder about the effects of music and the way it allowed a link to people I didn't know. A bridge for sharing the deeper feelings we all experience.

I've always said to audiences how important they are. You can pick up on the atmosphere within a nanosecond of walking on stage. I love that sense of expectation and the desire to listen and receive – it fired me up at every performance. Even with the largest audiences, you can create an intimacy that is truly memorable.

I remember once, while touring in Zimbabwe, a concert had unfortunately been planned on the same night as a big local school event. Instead of 400 people in the audience, I had roughly 30. I'd been up at the crack of dawn to catch a flight, I was tired, it was extremely hot in the dressing room and I wondered how on earth I was going to work up the energy to give my best. I needn't have worried. The moment I walked out and saw the expectant and enthusiastic faces of my tiny audience (including a small child in the front row), the adrenaline started pumping again. In fact, it was the best concert of the tour.

In the early 1990s I began to give spoken introductions during my recitals, to break down the invisible barrier than can exist between performer and audience. The atmosphere created when there is symbiotic connection is hard to define, yet it's intuitively, and mutually, experienced.

Since the pandemic, performers have had to learn to give their best 'virtually' without the essential ingredient of the audience. For me, this was the toughest thing to overcome. I was fortunate to give many concerts in December just before I retired from playing – and, without exception, the audiences said how much they had missed seeing performers live onstage. Many listeners were in tears because the power of live music was so overwhelming.

This shared experience of music spurs performers to greater heights, and the atmosphere created – the element of the unknown, the art of spontaneity – simply cannot be replaced or replicated.

Adapt to Survive

Like many professions, the music industry has had to square up to the challenges of social distancing. ARIANE TODES looks into some of the ways that orchestras have responded – creatively and digitally – in lockdown

An orchestra is by definition a gathering of people. These people sit together at close quarters for long periods, all the better to hear each other and respond to their conductor as one body. This proximity was never a hazard until last year, when Covid-19 began its rampage. The concert stage became one of its playfields.

As we look ahead to the second Proms season under pandemic conditions, the orchestral landscape has changed beyond recognition – from how these groups rehearse and perform to the ways they communicate and even the music they play. The crisis has certainly proved how flexible and adaptable musicians can be.

Lateral flow tests, temperature checks, one-way systems and hand-sanitising have become the new normal, as has social distancing. Music may fulfil our spiritual and emotional needs, but planning how it happens now largely comes down to bodily functions. Allowing enough time for loo breaks has become a priority, dictating both the structure of rehearsals and how programmes are planned – hence compact concerts without an interval have become the norm.

In the initial stages of the crisis, rules excluded wind and brass players, removing the dangers of their saliva, which they usually empty from their instruments onto the stage, so we heard a lot of string music. Lobbying by the industry brought back these sections, although they have to bring their own improvised spittoons.

New-style programmes are largely dictated by the logistics of the two-metre social-distancing rule and how many players it allows onstage. Unless orchestras can access large rehearsal spaces (the London Symphony Orchestra has LSO St Luke's and the Bournemouth Symphony Orchestra has the Lighthouse in Poole), they have to cut back on players, so out go full-strength performances of Bruckner and Mahler.

The two-metre rule also means that each string player has their own music stand rather than sharing in pairs (or 'desks'). After a lifetime of sitting closely together, this takes getting used to. Daniel Meyer, a Second Violinist in the BBC Symphony Orchestra, remembers the first rehearsal after lockdown, with only eight players in his section, rather than the usual 14: 'Normally you play off your desk partner, but that non-verbal communication is impossible when you're isolated. You are more reliant on the conductor, and it's very hard to work out how to grade your contribution – you have to play more soloistically, yet still be part of the ensemble.'

Violinist Kati Debretzeni describes playing again with the English Baroque Soloists and Monteverdi Choir after the long lay-off: 'It was a mixture of relief to be hearing music and all the emotions that came with playing in a group together. Then there was the shock of only hearing myself. How do you play as a section? Your ears are on stalks, and the stalks get longer and longer as you hear further in the distance.'

BBC National Orchestra of Wales viola player Laura Jayne Sinnerton says, 'It's much harder to feel and hear the physical cues you normally pick up from your section principal, concertmaster and colleagues. You can't rely on what you're hearing – if you do, you'll come in late, so it's a great leap of faith. You have to go with what you see on the podium. It feels lonely and exposed. You have to learn symphonies as if they're solo works.'

This has changed her way of working: 'I get hold of the scores now and get into the guts of each piece, because there isn't the security of being able to hear everyone else. You have to know the music better and it's helpful to know the whole context. Parts and scores are all available to us online in advance – this had already started to happen, but it's a resource we're using much more now.'

How does it feel to play without an audience? Last year's Last Night of the Proms was denied the usual audience revelry in the Royal Albert Hall, but Meyer admits there was one advantage: 'Trying to concentrate on the Last Night of the Proms is usually incredibly difficult, so from that point of view there were fewer things getting in the way. It was eerie playing in an empty hall, though,

▲ Safety at work: the socially distanced musicians of the Orchestra of the Age of Enlightenment onstage at last year's Proms

the lockdown challenge of learning the tuba – also sees the benefits: 'Covid has sped up the necessity of looking more at our online presence. Pop and rock music adapted quickly to online platforms such as Twitter, TikTok and Snapchat, but in classical music we can be a little shy. Maybe we don't think we're exciting enough or that what we do would work on modern platforms, but the interactions the orchestra has seen through our online presence have increased month on month. It's a great way to spread our love for this genre and for our passionate belief that education should be accessible to everyone.'

The lack of audience also changes the acoustic, which is a challenge for the conductor, especially in a piece such as Mozart's overture to *The Marriage of Figaro*, which opened the programme. Meyer says: 'You've got a big hall to fill and it's more resonant than normal because it doesn't have people in it. It's hard to find the right tempo to enable us all to hear each other and play together, but Dalia [Stasevska] managed to find exactly the right speed in rehearsal, which we hit in the evening.'

Of the positive aspects to emerge, one is that orchestras have discovered new ways of communicating with audiences, with players connecting directly with fans. The Royal Philharmonic Orchestra has had an active online presence with #RPOatHome, including playlists, quizzes and podcasts, and Co-Principal Cellist Jonathan Ayling has filmed a series describing his own journey with the Bach Cello Suites. Managing Director James Williams says, 'The pandemic has given an opportunity for individual voices, rather than just the larger group, to shine not only musically but also personality-wise. Audiences feel very connected, getting inside musicians' minds, processes and lives. It's been a valuable building exercise between audiences and musicians.'

In this era of 'big data', this activity may help to reshape orchestras' activities. Williams says, 'The focus on digital audiences has allowed us to gain a lot of information about their behaviour, which is much harder with a live audience. That will inform how we extend the journey of those audiences into the live experience and how we serve our immediate communities. It reminds us of the importance of diversity of programming and the need to think carefully about access, not just pushing content out, but thinking about how it matches the audience we want to reach.'

Some orchestras have used technology to ramp up their educational and community work, spreading the power of music across schools and care homes beyond the previous limits of space and time. BBC NOW has given school workshops across Wales. Sinnerton says, 'One day we gave separate workshops

so it was lovely having the BBC Singers, who applauded and gave us support, as we did when they performed.

Sinnerton, who has been busy on social media for BBC NOW – even setting herself

Together apart: double bass players of the London Symphony Orchestra – suitably distanced – warming up backstage at the Royal Albert Hall before performing at last year's Proms

with schools near Cardiff and Llandudno and in Flintshire. This wouldn't be possible without online.' The players have also used digital tools to mentor future professionals, as well as keeping up morale and playing standards – players of the viola section practise together (on mute) every morning on Zoom.

Without official technical or IT support, musicians have also become expert recording producers and curators. 'We've all had to evolve a whole new set of skills,' says Williams. 'Suddenly we had to become technicians and editors – and not just our staff, but our musicians as well. They were having to produce content on their own. We have also discovered musicians who can write and present fantastically.'

On the legal side, an unprecedented situation, combined with rules that have often seemed chaotic, has had implications for how the business works. Mark Pemberton, Director of the ABO, explains: 'For every rehearsal and concert, there is a supply chain of artists who come in and out of the country. The global traffic of conductors and soloists has ground to a halt, which has in turn tested the contracts that exist between a promoter, orchestra and artist manager. How do we revisit contracts to enable cancellations to happen in a way that's fair to everyone?'

The global halt has also raised existential questions, he says: 'If you want to put on a concert, it's easier to find conductors and soloists who are already here, rather than fly them in. The way in which orchestras work isn't particularly green. We accept that cultural exchange is a moral good and we value taking art and artists from one country to another, but we've had to be local during this period and that may continue. There may be more balance between nurturing homegrown talent while still bringing in stars from abroad when we need them.'

So far, most orchestras have weathered the storm. Without the UK Government's Cultural Recovery Fund and furlough scheme there might have been much more long-term damage, although the situation has been catastrophic for orchestral freelancers: according to ABO research, 30 per cent have had no financial support since the start of the crisis. And we're not out of the woods. 'The Government and scientists are very nervous about mass gatherings,' Pemberton says. 'It could be that most of the economy is allowed to reopen but that restrictions continue for the event sector, and the Government has switched off all its support measures – that's when we might have a problem.'

One can only hope and keep all fingers crossed. Certainly our screens have become a greater part of our musical lives than we might ever have imagined and fulfilled some of our needs. But, however sophisticated digital concerts become and whatever positive things have emerged from the crisis, we all long for the musicians and audiences to throng together at the Royal Albert Hall once more with collective excitement. ●

Ariane Todes is a music journalist and editor who has played in amateur orchestras for many years. She is a former editor of The Strad.

Northern Soul

How a lockdown project allowed the BBC Philharmonic to reflect its region and find new audiences in the process

During the pandemic, many of us have embraced new activities, whether baking sourdough bread or knitting. The Salford-based BBC Philharmonic turned to pop music and accidentally sparked a revolution.

The idea for the Great Northern Playlist started with the popularity of the videos the orchestra's players created in the first lockdown. By May 2020 there was an official challenge, hashtag and all, with breakfast presenters of 10 local BBC radio stations in the North of England putting out the call for suggestions of songs that spoke to their region. The players were then given two weeks to arrange, perform and edit the 10 chosen songs.

The resulting videos ranged from Chris Rea's 'On the Beach' to Little Mix's 'Black Magic', by way of Soft Cell's 'Tainted Love'. What began as a morale-booster has turned into a game-changer, says the orchestra's General Manager, Simon Webb. 'We discovered two things: a new audience, which orchestras were not reaching, and a way of working that has enabled us to create totally different music: it isn't orchestral repertoire but it's completely orchestral.'

Ahead of the Curve

Pushing on the boundaries of categorisation, Moses Sumney's music is set for an orchestral reinterpretation at this year's Proms. AMMAR KALIA goes to the source of the singer-songwriter's 'inherent multiplicity' and meets his latest collaborator, Jules Buckley

here is an inherent multiplicity to Moses Sumney's music. Since the release of his debut EP, *Mid-City Island*, in 2014, the Ghanaian-American singer-songwriter has defied categorisation, moving at turns through the sweetened R&B falsetto of the likes of Marvin Gaye, to raw introspective narration and luscious instrumental arrangements. His songs express the fraught emotional possibilities between yearning and satisfaction, and between how we see ourselves and how we are seen by others.

It is an enticing sound that has seen Sumney garner critical acclaim from *The Guardian*, *The New York Times* and *Rolling Stone*, as well as ensuring collaborations with artists including James Blake, Bon Iver and The National's Bryce Dessner. Sumney has established himself as a fiercely independent artist, directing many of his own videos and writing every one of his lyrics. The manifestation of numerous, sometimes opposing, elements within Sumney's music speaks of his journeying existence.

Born in California, he relocated to his parents' native Ghana aged 10, before returning to the USA at 16. During this back-and-forth, he began to write his own *a cappella* music, organically developing the intricate, multi-tracked harmonies that so warmly envelop his later work.

▲ Moses Sumney strikes a pose while on a visit to his parents' native Ghana; he spent almost six years living in the country as a child

With only his voice for creative company, Sumney took a typically independent route into the wider music industry. Eschewing the overtures of major record labels after the release of his lo-fi, self-recorded debut EP, Sumney instead embedded himself within LA's alternative indie music scene. Here he befriended and often musically accompanied the likes of folk auteur Sufjan Stevens, TV On The Radio's Dave Sitek, and Solange Knowles, steadily growing a loyal, grass-roots following with the ensuing release of his *Lamentations* EP in 2016 on independent outfit Jagjaguwar.

As a consequence of his time spent in LA, Sumney's pool of possible collaborators had been widening but still, when it came to the release of his debut LP, *Aromanticism*, in 2017, his music radiated the cocooned vulnerability of creative isolation. Comprising delicate compositions wrought from a whispered yearning for emotional connection, *Aromanticism* is an album that is as tender as it is self-assured. On standout singles 'Plastic' and 'Doomed', for instance, Sumney's falsetto meanders through insistence to fragility, defiance and ambivalence. Here is a searching multiplicity in all its musical and emotional forms – one that found itself a global audience and critical acclaim, appearing on several 'best of 2017' lists from *Pitchfork* to *The New York Times*.

On Sumney's 2020 follow-up, the double album *græ*, he blossomed from *Aromanticism*'s self-imposed isolation into embracing the tentative multitudes it contained. As evoked by the album

title's ligature, its two-part release and the playful oppositions of its track titles – 'jill/jack', 'Neither/Nor' – on *græ* Sumney allowed his musical moods to be brash, joyous and purposefully obtrusive, meandering from spoken-word interludes to rumbling distortion and earworming melodies. His falsetto often graduating to a full-throated roar, in this newfound, experimental confidence we hear the sprawling messiness of living itself. It is as if Sumney explores different musical forms on *græ* to enact the complicated psychology of identity and its refusal to be boxed in. 'This was the core tenet of *græ*: exploring the isolation that comes from staking out the middle ground, or what I call the "Great In-Between"', Sumney wrote this year in *Wonderland*. 'It's recognising that the world is neither this nor that, and neither am I.'

In this exploration, Sumney finds ripe material for his upcoming Proms collaboration with conductor Jules Buckley and the BBC Symphony Orchestra. Sumney and Buckley had been in touch for several years, trying to find a way to work together, before the opportunity of the Proms presented itself. 'Moses is such a unique artist and he is so deserving of a broader audience that comes with a festival like the Proms,' Buckley says. 'He has an incredibly original sound – a sweeping, cinematic and detailed production – that is so exciting to bring into an orchestral context.' Drawing on work from Sumney's entire back catalogue, the pair are producing a performance that aims to combine the free-flowing state of

For Buckley, one track in particular stands out from Sumney's work: 'Virile' from *græ*. 'It's one of the greatest tunes I've ever heard. It's a difficult one to approach but we're building the concept together to make it into something new, and that is really the essence of what we're trying to achieve,' he says. 'I want parts of this show to feel like you can't necessarily define what the sound is – rather, it meanders between the acoustic and the electronic.'

The collaboration is also a prime example of what Buckley set out to achieve when he became Creative Artist in Association with the BBC Symphony Orchestra in 2019. 'This concert epitomises what orchestras are doing today and it helps to expand the reach of the orchestral sound,' he says. 'Programmes like this one push people out of their comfort zones – and that has always been a major element of my work.'

'Moses's music feels like new music. It is uncompromising and unique, and that is what makes it so exciting,' Buckley adds. And in its reinterpretation within an orchestral context it takes on another facet to that ever-developing multiplicity. There is no certainty nor resting point when it comes to creative self-expression, Sumney seems to say through his work, only the ever-new journeying-on, in all its inspiring and nascent forms. ●

Ammar Kalia is Global Music Critic at *The Guardian*. He has published a collection of poetry and an accompanying album, *Kintsugi: Jazz Poems for Musicians Alive and Dead*, and is currently working on his debut novel.

Sumney's close-knit and improvisational band with the structured maximalism of an orchestral arrangement, all serving to blur the boundaries between voice and production, while retaining a sense of clarity. As Sumney told *Pitchfork* last year: 'In order for something to be artful and valid and full of meaning, it doesn't have to be esoteric, obscured or mysterious.'

Having previously worked with an astonishing range of artists, including Laura Marling, Chaka Khan and Anoushka Shankar, Buckley still found Sumney's music particularly challenging to reimagine. 'It takes a while to unlock the key sound-concepts of his work,' Buckley says. 'The frequencies that Moses is covering in his voice – from the falsetto element to the virtuosic nature of his vocal delivery – mean we have to make sure that the instrumentation is not getting in the way of that. The vocal is king, so we have to find the frequency ranges that allow the orchestra to add another dimension to Moses's work.'

Sumney and his vocal presence are certainly central to any project he touches. He displays an auteurship in everything from the *græ* album cover, depicting his naked body draped over a glistening rock like a newly discovered geological element, to his self-directed videos of writhing choreography for tracks 'Bless Me' and 'Cut Me'. In their work together he and Buckley will similarly ensure their process retains Sumney's creative authority at its forefront, honing their set-list from opposite sides of the Atlantic via a series of shared playlists.

Explorers by instinct: Jules Buckley helps sitarist and composer Anoushka Shankar to reimagine her own music with the Britten Sinfonia at last year's Proms

Moses Sumney Meets Jules Buckley and the BBC Symphony Orchestra
21 AUGUST

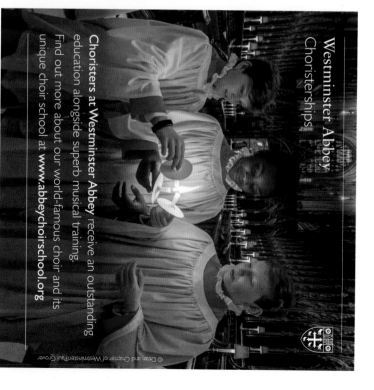

Renaissance Resplendence

Five hundred years after his death, **CAROLINE GILL** charts the rise of Josquin des Prez, whose rapturous multi-voice music combines colour with reverence and emotion with purity

ver the course of the 15th century, Gregorian chant – the single-line Latin songs dominant in Western liturgical music – began to evolve into multi-voice music in the cathedrals of northern Europe. In this new style, a single line of chant (the *cantus firmus*) was borrowed from the liturgy to form the basis of music for multiple voices, around which the singers would also improvise. By the end of the century, the skilled singer-composers of northern Europe started to travel south in pursuit of job offers from, among others, the grand courts and chapels of Italy. Josquin was one of these. He was known by many names – among them Josquin Lebloitte, Gossequin de Condé, Josquin des Prez and Josquinus Pratensis – so it's hardly surprising he's more generally known as just 'Josquin'.

This uncertainty over his name is only one of several unknowns that have played a role in Josquin's altogether misty history. We do not know what he looked like: a single woodcut is the source of most of his portraits, despite a lingering suggestion that he may also have sat for Leonardo da Vinci's famous unidentified *Portrait of a Musician* when he was working in Milan in the 1480s. The only example we know of his handwriting was the autograph he apparently gouged into the ceiling of the Sistine Chapel choir

loft after joining the papal chapel choir in 1489. Not knowing his movements in any detail over the course of his career also inevitably means that we cannot be certain that every piece ascribed to Josquin is, in fact, by Josquin. There is a remarkable amount of surviving anecdotal evidence, however, and without exception the accounts of music theorists, pupils of his pupils and fellow composers describe him as an irascible, exacting and excessively self-critical personality.

In 1502 the collection of Masses, *Misse Josquin*, rolled off the brand-new presses of Ottaviano Petrucci, creating widespread dissemination of Josquin's work and garnering him an impressive reputation. This new status as a first-generation published composer placed him at a cultural crossroads where art music was beginning to be shared across countries, and where composers could achieve a lasting identity via printed scores rather than mouldering manuscripts. The singular ingenuity of Josquin's music also began to catch people's attention once it appeared in Petrucci's collections: in the same year that Josquin first appeared in print an agent for Duke Ercole I of Ferrara, Girolamo da Sestola, fought off a rival to find a new court composer for the Duke, securing Josquin for the post at an extortionate salary of 200 florins. 'By having Josquin,' said Sestola, 'I want to place a crown on this chapel of ours.'

Josquin's music has been consistently identified as singularly accomplished, varied and unpredictable. Ravishing melodies, complicated techniques, unusual intervals and sensitivity to the text were all defined as emblems of Josquin's style and pulled out of his work for use in the later 16th-century 'parody Masses' of composers such as Cipriano de Rore (whose *Missa Praeter rerum seriem* is built around the musical motifs of Josquin's motet of the same name) – a form in which homage was paid, through quotation, to composers whose reputations were already sealed.

More attention has been paid to Josquin over the past 30 years as musicologists and performers have explored the mystifying variety of his skill, artifice and invention. Of the 340 pieces currently ascribed to him, some will likely be the work of other, lost, masters or mistresses of polyphony. Perhaps in the end, though, it is exactly this uncertainty that continues to engage us, 500 years after his death. And so, through musicology and performance – as well as through musical borrowings in the new compositions that push the boundaries of creativity ever wider – the search to reconcile the elusive beauty of his music with the opacity of his historical picture goes on. ●

Caroline Gillis is a journalist and critic who appears on Radio 3's *Record Review*. She is a visiting lecturer at London's Royal College of Music and pursues research on Italian Renaissance music at the University of Huddersfield.

9 AUGUST

Praeter rerum seriem; Benedicta es, caelorum regina; Inviolata, integra et casta es

19 AUGUST

Qui habitat in adiutorio altissimi (a 24)

▲ The Church of Saint-Géry in Cambrai, northern France, where Josquin was a chorister in 1466

There once was a ship that put to sea …

In the year social media was awash with shanties and other sea-songs – a traditional theme of the Last Night of the Proms – writer HORATIO CLARE surveys the currents of romance, harsh reality and community spirit that accompany life on the waves

ur common reaction to the changing of the world began, as each Prom will end, in music and applause. Do you remember the images of a dim back street at night, unsteadily filmed on a mobile, and echoing voices shaking with feeling, joining in a ballad? People around the world burst into tears at the footage of quarantined Italians singing from their windows and balconies. In Spain, Israel, Iraq, Lebanon, France, the USA and other countries, thousands came out and sang. Next came the applause. From India to Turkey to Canada, and everywhere in Britain, millions clapped for the carers of the first wave. Then, in the depths of the second wave and a cruel northern winter, Nathan Evans, a 26-year-old Scottish postman, uploaded a video of him singing the whaling song 'Wellerman' onto TikTok.

The film is black-and-white. Evans, in the corner of a room, wearing a global lockdown uniform – a hoodie and beanie hat – could be anywhere. Fixing the camera with a furrowed gaze, keeping time on a drum, he sings. *There once was a ship that put to sea, the name of the ship was the 'Billy of Tea' …*

Duets, collaborations and remixes flooded the world's screens. Most were recorded by young people, often in cramped spaces – the kind of small compass in which so many, and so very many of the young, endured their lockdowns. Many contributors sang into little mics dangling from their earphones.

Social media sensations can be many things but they are seldom moving in the way this is. As Samuel Barber's *Adagio for Strings* in the aftermath of 9/11, as Tony Walsh's poem 'This is the Place' in response to the Manchester Arena bombing, so our trauma now found a music that, for millions, seemed to answer it. A young Scot on a Chinese platform singing a song from the 19th-century whaling fleet of New Zealand spoke, suddenly, to the time.

It is partly the way Evans does it – gravely, longingly, as the song demands – and partly that he looks and sounds so right for it. I travelled the trading seas, writing about the seafarers upon whose work our daily world relies. Many are young men not at all unlike Evans, be they Filipino, Chinese or Indonesian. I found them serious and kind, and often battling, far from home and family, deep loneliness and grating worry. They hold their fears at bay or bury them as they sail their ships, and all our food and goods, from port to port.

The rallying, nostalgic and heroic character of music inspired by the sea begins in isolation, endurance and defiance. This, tangibly, is the art of people who needed music to bring them together, to help them work in rhythm, to raise their spirits, or brace their souls with hope. It faces down the terrors of the deep.

With over half the world's population having experienced lockdown, billions of us now know something of what that facing-down, alone or in small groups, is really like.

As you listen at the Last Night of the Proms to the 'Hornpipe' in Henry Wood's *Fantasia on British Sea-Songs*, compiled to commemorate the centenary of the Battle of Trafalgar, it may be easier, this year, to link it to real young men dancing in gay defiance of harsh conditions and an environment that switches from endless beauty to brutal threat.

Captain Cook had his crews dance the hornpipe for the same reasons we have been urging ourselves and each other to walks, work-outs and yoga: to stay fit, yes, but equally to manufacture cheer and well-being out of cramped and apprehensive adversity.

Although sailors took to the hornpipe – Samuel Pepys refers to it as 'The Jig of the Ship' in his diary – it may well have begun in folk traditions on land. Shanties, meanwhile, come straight from the sea.

Soon may the Wellerman come, to bring us sugar and tea and rum, Nathan Evans and his vast accompanying choirs sing. It is very hard not to join in, even if TikTok and memes are not for you, thanks to the song's yearning melancholy and spirit of resistance: *One day, when the tonguin' is done, we'll take our leave and go …*

It is thought that the song's unknown composer on the whaling ship may have been one of the younger of the crew. He

▲ Cold reality: a whaling crew capsized in the Arctic (wood engraving, c1833)

of phlegmatic humour, born from deep seriousness in a perilous environment, that we found in ourselves and in each other, wherever in the world we are, as the storms of the pandemic broke over us. I heard those tones repeatedly on telephones, on Zoom calls, in shops, in the conversations of passers-by.

Britain, an archipelago on the edge of the continental shelf, has become strikingly aware of its islanded nature. For a while, perhaps, we held onto our maritime history as heritage, something proud but increasingly misty. Those mists have cleared. Ships, ports, customs and resupply have always mattered, and suddenly we all know how much.

The working oceans have been driven back by modernity. Where once the sea was the heart of many of the greatest cities of the world, now it is confined behind the high fences of container ports, relegated to the out-of-sight, out-of-mind world upon which so much of globalisation relies. In this unconsidered, alternative world, Felixstowe is a small capital but Rotterdam a megacity and the Dover Strait a stretch of the world's Fifth Avenue, which runs all the way through Suez to the Strait of Malacca and on to the Panama Canal.

This parallel place sustains everything we call normality, and its importance to everything we need and make has only grown. 'You can tell how the economy is going,' a pilot at Felixstowe told me, 'by the height of the ship in the water.' Pilots join container ships by scrambling up a ladder. When British exports are low or global trade is slow, it is, as he put it, 'a fair old climb – quite exciting in a gale'. It was this kind of toughness, this kind

Towards the end of my travels with seafarers, I felt that this earth is a ship and all of us are sailors – from the lowliest wipers and oilers to the engineers and captains, we are all of them, all at once. If it was a romantic sentiment at the time, it does not seem so now. I learnt that crews come from many nations, occupying different stations in the ship's hierarchy; and, though they live side by side, in their cabins they are deeply solitary. It is only when a ship faces peril or disaster that a crew is moulded together, and experiences as one something that only they will ever understand.

Through these times, through the shared emotions of these months, as billions faced an identical threat, perhaps for the first time in history, it was suddenly extraordinarily easy to imagine being in each other's cabins, living each other's lives. We are all in one ship, and we have known it. And so we sing, and we applaud each other, like sailors of one sea. ●

Horatio Clare's books include Running for the Hills: A Memoir, Down to the Sea in Ships *– in which he travelled with crews on container ships – and, most recently,* Heavy Light: A Journey through Madness, Mania & Healing. *He has broadcast on Radio 3 and writes regularly for the* Financial Times, The Spectator *and* Condé Nast Traveller.

Wood Fantasia on British Sea-Songs

LAST NIGHT OF THE PROMS • 11 SEPTEMBER

The industrial scale of modern ocean life: a container ship in the Port of Felixstowe

The Proms on Radio, TV and Online

Last year, despite difficult circumstances, more than 15 million people experienced the Proms from home via radio, TV or online. Such a unique reach reflects the main aim of the festival: to bring the best of classical music to the widest possible audience. This year, with every Prom broadcast live on BBC Radio 3 and 20 Proms available on TV and BBC iPlayer, experiencing an unforgettable summer of music has never been easier.

Listen

Hear every Prom live on BBC Radio 3 and on the BBC Sounds app, where you can listen on demand until 11 October. Also listen out for Proms-themed editions of Radio 3's *In Tune* and *Record Review*.

Watch

Jan Younghusband, Head of BBC Music TV Commissioning, says: 'We are thrilled to be back this year, bringing 20 concerts to our audiences across BBC One, Two

and Four, which will be available on iPlayer for 30 days after the Last Night of the Proms. Our TV coverage will focus on showcasing the wealth of new talent, as well as interviews with leading stars and experts, bringing you up close to what is happening in the classical world as we emerge from the pandemic. There will also be special contributions to the Last Night filmed around the UK by our BBC colleagues. After one of the most difficult years in our industry's history, we are delighted to welcome artists to the Royal Albert Hall for what promises to be a superb summer of music-making.'

Online

Given the changeable nature of the UK's Covid-19 regulations, make sure you visit bbc.co.uk/proms for the most up-to-date information on Proms events, including what's on, how to buy tickets, social distancing and safety updates, and full details of how to watch and listen. •

> **66** With the whole-hearted support of the wonderful medium of broadcasting, I feel that I am at last on the threshold of realising my lifelong ambition of truly democratising the message of music, and making its beneficent effect universal.

Henry Wood in 1927, as the BBC began its first radio broadcasts of the Proms

🐦 @bbcproms   f @theproms   📷 @bbc_proms   #bbcproms

BBC SOUNDS   BBC iPlayer

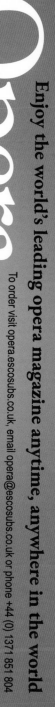

EVERY PROM LIVE ON BBC RADIO 3

Then continue enjoying live performances all year round with 'Radio 3 in Concert', weeknights at 7.30pm

LISTEN ANYTIME on the **BBC Sounds app**

Season Overview

This is your guide to the six-week season of concerts at the Royal Albert Hall and Cadogan Hall. It includes provisional programme details and Spotlight interviews with selected artists.

The information in these pages was correct at the time of going to press (late April). Programmes will be subject to alteration in response to the Government's evolving coronavirus regulations.

Before booking or attending any events, for up-to-date details – including listings, pricing, accessibility, social distancing, refunds, start-times, intervals and BBC TV broadcasts – please visit the BBC Proms website: bbc.co.uk/proms

We look forward to bringing you a summer of world-class music-making.

On Radio, TV and Online

 Every Prom is broadcast live on BBC Radio 3 and available on BBC Sounds until 11 October

 20 Proms are broadcast on BBC TV and available on BBC iPlayer until 11 October

Booking

Online
bbc.co.uk/promstickets
or royalalberthall.com

By phone
on 020 7070 4441
(from 9.00am on 26 June) †

General booking
Booking will take place in two Booking Periods this year, opening on 26 June and 17 July respectively. For further booking, venue and access information, see pages 113–115.

† CALL COSTS
Standard geographic charges from landlines and mobiles apply. All calls may be recorded and monitored for training and quality-control purposes.

Proms 2021 Calendar

Mon	**2 August** 1.00pm (P@CH1) Zemlinsky, Brahms Collins, Brendel, McHale 7.00pm • Purcell/ Stokowski, Ogonek, Saint-Saëns, Brahms BBC NOW/Chan	**9 August** 1.00pm (P@CH2) Josquin, Calvisius, Willaert, Lusitano Marian Consort/McCleery 7.30pm • Bates, Elgar, Janáček	Moser, Bournemouth SO/Karabits	**16 August** 1.00pm (P@CH3) • Haydn, Simpson	Marmen Quartet 7.30pm • To Soothe the Aching Heart Soloists, BBC Philharmonic/ Glassberg
Tue	**3 August** 7.30pm • Schubert, Milch- Sheriff, Beethoven Danker, BBC Philharmonic/Weilber	**10 August** 7.30pm • Byström BBC Philharmonic/ Storgårds	**17 August** 7.30pm • Górecki, Finnis, Eastman, Tabakova, Horovitz Esfahani, Manchester Collective/Singh
Wed	**4 August** 7.30pm • Vaughan Williams, Respighi, Mendelssohn Shoji, RPO/V. Petrenko	**11 August** 7.30pm • Rachmaninov, Stravinsky Service, Kolesnikov, Aurora Orchestra/Collon	**18 August** 7.30pm • Nubya Garcia
Thu	**5 August** 7.30pm • Gipps, Adès CBSO/Gražinytė-Tyla	**12 August** 7.30pm • Stravinsky, Walton, Bach/Goldmann, Hindemith Isserlis, LPO/Jurowski	**19 August** 7.30pm • Josquin, Byrd, Williams, Stravinsky, Sweelinck, Muhly, Feshareki Feshareki, Byrne, BBC Singers/Jeannin
Fri	**30 July** 7.30pm • First Night of the Proms 2021: Vaughan Williams, Poulenc, MacMillan	BBC Singers, BBC SO/Stasevska	**6 August** 7.30pm • Pergolesi, Stravinsky Sampson, Mead, Hulett, Shibambu, BBC SSO/Carneiro	**13 August** 7.30pm BBC SO/Davis	**20 August** 7.30pm *Please see bbc.co.uk/proms* *for updates*
Sat	**31 July** 7.30pm • The Golden Age of Broadway BBC CO/Balcombe	**7 August** 7.30pm • Jurd, Prokofiev, Beethoven Benedetti, NYOGB/Heyward	**14 August** 7.30pm • Prokofiev, Bach, Mozart, Shostakovich Ólafsson, Philharmonia Orchestra/Rouvali	**21 August** 7.30pm • Moses Sumney Meets Jules Buckley and the BBC Symphony Orchestra
Sun	**1 August** matinee • Organ Recital 7.30pm • Mozart Scottish Chamber Orchestra/Emelyanychev	**8 August** 7.00pm • Thomas, Ives, Dvořák BBC NOW/Bancroft	**15 August** 7.00pm	Selaocoe, Lagnawi, Chesaba, BBC NOW/Rundell	**22 August** 7.30pm • Stravinsky LSO/Rattle

23 August
1.00pm & P@CH4
Piazzolla, Ramírez,
Walker, Shibe
7.30pm *Please see bbc.co.uk/ proms for updates*

24 August
7.30pm • Coleridge-Taylor,
Sowande, Price
J. Kanneh-Mason,
Chineke! Orchestra/Bovell

25 August
7.30pm • Vivaldi, Piazzolla/
Desyatnikov
Academy of St Martin in the
Fields/Bell

26 August
7.30pm • Lewis, Beethoven
Crowe, BBC SSO/Volkov

27 August
7.30pm • Bray, Walton, Arnold
BBC SO/Oramo

28 August
7.30pm • Bartók Roots
Kopatchinskaja,
BBC SSO/Dausgaard

29 August
7.00pm • Saint-Saëns
(Family Prom)
Kanneh-Mason family et al.

30 August
1.00pm P@CH5
Saint-Saëns, Gipps, Dutilleux,
Poulenc, Bozza
Leleux, Le Sage
7.30pm • Knussen, Purcell/
Benjamin, Ravel, Benjamin
Aimard, Mahler CO/Benjamin

31 August
4.00pm • Wagner: Tristan and
Isolde
Glyndebourne Festival Opera,
LPO/Ticciati

1 September
7.30pm • Handel, Bach
Hallenberg, Monteverdi Choir,
English Baroque Soloists/
Gardiner

2 September
7.30pm • 20th-Century British
Film Music
BBC CO/Tovey

3 September
7.30pm | Gerstein,
BBC SO/Bychkov

4 September
matinee • Organ Recital:
Saint-Saëns, Liszt | Trotter
7.30pm • J. Strauss, Berg, Ravel,
Korngold | Persson,
Sinfonia of London/Wilson

5 September
7.30pm • Dvořák, Mason,
R. Strauss, Hindemith
S. Kanneh-Mason,
RLPO/Hindoyan

6 September
1.00pm P@CH6
Pauline Viardot and Her Circle
Nikolovska, Martineau
7.30pm • Glass, Moussa
McVinnie, BBC Concert
Orchestra/Helsing

7 September
7.30pm • Chin, Beethoven,
Saint-Saëns
Grosvenor, Lapwood,
Hallé/Elder

8 September
7.30pm
*Please see bbc.co.uk/proms
for updates*

9 September
7.30pm • Bach: St Matthew
Passion
Jackson, Hymas, Williams,
Finley, Arcangelo Chorus,
Arcangelo/Cohen

10 September
7.30pm
*Please see bbc.co.uk/proms
for updates*

11 September
7.30pm • Last Night of the
Proms 2021: Wood, Arne/
Sargent, Elgar, Parry/Elgar,
Trad.
Skelton, Sidorova,
BBC Singers, BBC SO/Oramo

Key
P@CH Proms at ... Cadogan Hall

**These are provisional
listings. Please
check the Proms
website for the latest
information:
bbc.co.uk/proms**

Friday 30 July

7.30pm • Royal Albert Hall

First Night of the Proms 2021

Programme to include:

Vaughan Williams Serenade to Music — 15'

Poulenc Organ Concerto — 22'

Sir James MacMillan new work — c8'
BBC co-commission: world premiere

Daniel Hyde *organ*

BBC Singers
BBC Symphony Orchestra
Dalia Stasevska *conductor*

Dalia Stasevska, the BBC Symphony Orchestra's Principal Guest Conductor, leads a First Night featuring Vaughan Williams's ravishing *Serenade to Music* – written to celebrate Proms founder-conductor Henry Wood's 50 years on the podium and premiered by him at his jubilee concert in the Royal Albert Hall in 1938. Poulenc's Organ Concerto is a piquant foil, showcasing the instrument in a vivid play of light and shade, and Sir James MacMillan offers a new work to launch the new season. See '*A Gift to the Nation'*, *pages 36–41*.

MAXIM EMELYANYCHEV • 1 AUGUST

MICHAEL COLLINS • 2 AUGUST

Saturday 31 July

7.30pm • Royal Albert Hall

The Golden Age of Broadway

BBC Concert Orchestra
Richard Balcombe *conductor*

Soloists to be announced

Smell the greasepaint and feel the blaze of those Broadway lights, as the BBC Concert Orchestra whisks you away for a night at the musicals. The toe-tapping favourites include overtures and tear-jerkers from Broadway giants including Cole Porter, Jerome Kern, George Gershwin and Richard Rodgers, all performed by the ever-versatile BBC Concert Orchestra – and some special guest soloists.

ADRIAN BRENDEL • 2 AUGUST

Sunday 1 August

matinee • Royal Albert Hall

Organ Recital

Soloist to be announced

When the Royal Albert Hall was officially opened in 1871, it welcomed its first audience to the sound of the mighty 'Father' Willis organ – then powered by two steam engines. We celebrate the Hall's 150th-anniversary year with a recital showcasing the power and range of an instrument whose

These are provisional listings for the 2021 BBC Proms season.

Please note that changes in the Government's Covid-19 regulations may affect programmes, artists, start-times and audience numbers.

Please check the Proms website for the latest information: bbc.co.uk/proms

ELIM CHAN • 2 AUGUST

SEE PAGES 113–115 FOR BOOKING INFORMATION

9,999 pipes would stretch nine miles if laid end to end, an organ that has been played by celebrated recitalists and rock legends alike. See 'A Gift to the Nation', pages 36–41.

Sunday 1 August

7.30pm • Royal Albert Hall

Mozart

Symphony No. 39 in E flat major	29'
Symphony No. 40 in G minor	30'
Symphony No. 41 in C major, 'Jupiter'	31'

Scottish Chamber Orchestra
Maxim Emelyanychev conductor

Composed within just two months in the summer of 1788, Mozart's three final symphonies together form a musical sequence that explores all sides of humanity; No. 39 offers a grand introduction, its fanfares and dances setting the scene, before we're plunged into the dark drama of the Symphony No. 40, and finally emerge into the sunlight of the 'Jupiter' Symphony, with its dazzling fugal finale. The Scottish Chamber Orchestra is conducted by its dynamic Principal Conductor Maxim Emelyanychev.

Monday 2 August

PROMS AT CADOGAN HALL ❶
1.00pm • Cadogan Hall

Zemlinsky Clarinet Trio in D minor, Op. 3		27'
Brahms Clarinet Trio in A minor, Op. 114		25'

Michael Collins clarinet
Adrian Brendel cello
Michael McHale piano

Celebrated British clarinettist Michael Collins is joined by cellist Adrian Brendel and pianist Michael McHale to celebrate the 150th anniversary of Austrian composer Alexander von Zemlinsky. Charged with fin de siècle intensity and taut musical drama, the young Zemlinsky's Clarinet Trio was much influenced

Monday 2 August

7.00pm • Royal Albert Hall

Purcell, arr. Stokowski Dido and Aeneas – 'When I am laid in earth' (Dido's Lament)	4'
Elizabeth Ogonek Cloudline *BBC co-commission: world premiere*	c15'
Saint-Saëns Cello Concerto No. 1 in A minor	19'
Brahms Symphony No. 4 in E minor	39'

BBC National Orchestra of Wales
Elim Chan conductor

Soloist to be announced

Musical borrowings, reworkings and reinventions run through this season's Proms. The invisible thread linking tonight's concert really begins with Bach. A lilting chaconne from his Cantata No. 150 underpins the finale of Brahms's Symphony No. 4, and the latter's elegant synthesis of heart and head is itself the inspiration for American composer Elizabeth Ogonek's Cloudline, a lyrical homage to ancient musical forms and techniques. The chaconne's repeating patterns are echoed elsewhere in the circling bass line of Purcell's powerful Lament from Dido and Aeneas. Award-winning conductor Elim Chan conducts the BBC National Orchestra of Wales. See 'Plunder Enlightening', pages 42–47.

20 Proms on BBC TV and available on BBC iPlayer

by Brahms, at whose recommendation it was published. A contemporary said of Brahms's own Trio in A minor that 'it is as though the instruments are in love with each other.' With its graceful waltz of an intermezzo and dashing finale with hints of Gypsy swagger, it's a musical love affair played out in glorious technicolour.

Spotlight on …

Dalia Stasevska • 30 July

When Dalia Stasevska made her debut as Principal Guest Conductor of the BBC Symphony Orchestra at the 2019 Proms, she probably expected, two years down the line, to have spent lots of time in London. For obvious reasons, that hasn't yet happened. 'Because of the lockdowns, we haven't had a chance to do many public concerts together,' she explains. 'Just one in the Barbican, two at the Proms and a few at the Maida Vale Studios. I'm still waiting to get fully immersed in the role.'

Stasevska calls this year's First Night of the Proms – which she'll be leading from the podium – a 'new beginning.' And not just for her and the BBC SO. After a disastrous year for the live music industry, this First Night – with the hope of an in-person audience – has taken on a symbolic hue of renewal. What do you need to consider when programming such a significant event? 'Dramaturgy is very important,' Stasevska says. 'You want to create a sense of celebration, with new works and commissions. But you also need a strong theme running through the programme.'

And, in her two Proms performances so far, what has she learnt from conducting in the cavernous Arena of the Royal Albert Hall? 'In every space you have to adapt very fast to the acoustics. And, because this one is so big, it has its own particular demands. Luckily there are many pairs of ears listening, helping to balance things out!'

by Japanese violinist Sayaka Shoji for Respighi's *Concerto gregoriano* – a spiritual serenade in which the soloist becomes a wordless cantor, whose plainsong-inspired melodies soar over the orchestra. Two more tributes to the musical past complete the programme: Vaughan Williams's haunting *Fantasia on a Theme by Thomas Tallis* takes inspiration from Tudor polyphony, while Mendelssohn's youthful 'Reformation' Symphony climaxes in Martin Luther's stirring chorale 'A mighty fortress is our God'. See *'Plunder Enlightening', pages 42–47.*

Tuesday 3 August

7.30pm • Royal Albert Hall

Schubert Symphony No. 2 in B flat major · 29'

Ella Milch-Sheriff The Eternal Stranger · 15'
BBC co-commission: UK premiere

Beethoven Symphony No. 4 in B flat major · 34'

Eli Danker *actor*

BBC Philharmonic
Omer Meir Wellber *conductor*

Beethoven is at the centre of a musical web connecting the 17-year-old Schubert's precocious, vivacious Symphony No. 2 – not only written in the elder composer's shadow, but quoting him directly – and Ella Milch-Sheriff's *The Eternal Stranger*, interweaving and reimagining fragments of Beethoven with the Middle Eastern colours and traditions of Israel. Dedicated to the BBC Philharmonic's Chief Conductor, Omer Meir Wellber, it sits alongside Beethoven's own Symphony No. 4, the composer's slender, graceful answer to the weightier symphonies that frame it. *See 'Plunder Enlightening', pages 42–47.*

OMER MEIR WELLBER • 3 AUGUST

VASILY PETRENKO • 4 AUGUST

Wednesday 4 August

7.30pm • Royal Albert Hall

Vaughan Williams Fantasia on a Theme by Thomas Tallis · 15'

Respighi Concerto gregoriano · 30'

Mendelssohn Symphony No. 5 in D major, 'Reformation' · 27'

Sayaka Shoji *violin*

Royal Philharmonic Orchestra
Vasily Petrenko *conductor*

Conductor Vasily Petrenko appears for the first time at the Proms in his new role as Music Director of the Royal Philharmonic Orchestra. They are joined

MIRGA GRAŽINYTĖ-TYLA • 5 AUGUST

NICOLA BENEDETTI • 7 AUGUST

Thursday 5 August

7.30pm • Royal Albert Hall

Programme to include:

Gipps Symphony No. 2 in B major   21'

Thomas Adès The Exterminating
Angel Symphony   20'
London premiere

City of Birmingham Symphony Orchestra
Mirga Gražinytė-Tyla *conductor*

The City of Birmingham Symphony Orchestra
and Music Director Mirga Gražinytė-Tyla champion
the music of a too-long neglected composer.
A pupil of Vaughan Williams, Ruth Gipps started
her career as an oboist with what was then the
City of Birmingham Orchestra in 1944, before
becoming established as a composer. Her Symphony
No. 2 takes a wide-screen, cinematic view of the
Second World War, embracing exhilaration, anxiety
and, finally, ecstatic rejoicing. Conflict of a very
different kind runs through *The Exterminating Angel
Symphony* by Thomas Adès (50 this year), inspired
by Louis Buñuel's Surrealist film. See *'An Indomitable
Maverick'*, pages 52–54.

BBC Scottish Symphony Orchestra to mark
the 50th anniversary of the composer's death with a
concert pairing the composer's ballet *Pulcinella* –
a witty, charming take on Baroque dance and
commedia dell'arte – with the heart-rending *Stabat
mater* by Pergolesi, whose music inspired it. See
'Plunder Enlightening', pages 42–47; *'Post Progressive'*,
pages 56–60.

Saturday 7 August

7.30pm • Royal Albert Hall

Laura Jurd new work   c8'
London premiere

Prokofiev Violin Concerto No. 2
in G minor   26'

Beethoven Symphony No. 3
in E flat major, 'Eroica'   47'

Nicola Benedetti *violin*

National Youth Orchestra of Great Britain
Jonathon Heyward *conductor*

Rising star Jonathon Heyward conducts the talented
teenagers of the National Youth Orchestra of
Great Britain in one of the all-time symphonic
greats. Propelling the symphony into the Romantic
age, Beethoven's 'Eroica' is a celebration of scope
and drama, a musical depiction of heroism that
surges with pioneering spirit. Nicola Benedetti is the
soloist in Prokofiev's Violin Concerto No. 2 with its
song-like slow movement – a work whose sardonic
wit is balanced by a new lyricism that would come
to dominate the composer's later works. The Prom
opens with a new NYOGB commission by British
composer, jazz trumpeter and former BBC Radio 3
New Generation Artist, Laura Jurd.

Friday 6 August

7.30pm • Royal Albert Hall

Pergolesi Stabat mater   39'

Stravinsky Pulcinella   40'

Carolyn Sampson *soprano*
Tim Mead *counter-tenor*
Benjamin Hulett *tenor*
Simon Shibambu *bass-baritone*

BBC Scottish Symphony Orchestra
Joana Carneiro *conductor*

Can a composer reuse the past and at the same
time move in a forward direction? It's the question
that goes to the heart of Igor Stravinsky's music –
works that often take their inspiration from historical
models but remain defiantly, distinctively modern.
Portuguese conductor Joana Carneiro joins the

Spotlight on ...

Joana Carneiro • 6 August

The last time Joana Carneiro conducted the
BBC Scottish Symphony Orchestra was at
the 2019 Edinburgh Festival. 'They were
so kind, so open and such great musicians,'
she says. 'I really had a wonderful time.' But
it's the way the orchestra 'champions this
continuous dialogue between the music of
the present and the music of the past' that
impresses her most. That same dialogue
sits front and centre at their upcoming
Prom, which places Stravinsky's *Pulcinella*
alongside a *Stabat mater* setting by
Pergolesi, the 18th-century composer who
sparked Stravinsky's neo-Classical period.

'From a musical point of view, it's extremely
interesting to have these pieces together:
the language that was the inspiration for
Pulcinella – one that marked the beginning
of a very important period of Stravinsky's
life – and *Pulcinella* itself.' But it's also an
opportunity for reflection: 'In a much
larger sense, it leads us to ask: how can we
learn from the past – the music, the times,
the history that we live – and look forward
to our lives as musicians in general?'

Carneiro has conducted *Pulcinella* before,
but this will be her first time performing
Pergolesi's *Stabat mater* – a challenge
she is relishing. 'I've conducted a lot of
other sacred music, but this setting is
particularly beautiful. The word-painting
has been a real discovery for me: the
sorrow and pain of the mother of Jesus is
set in such a dramatic and theatrical way.'

Sunday 8 August

7.00pm • Royal Albert Hall

Augusta Read Thomas
Dance Foldings   c13'
BBC commission: world premiere

Ives Three Places in New England
(Orchestral Set No. 1)   19'

Dvořák Symphony No. 9 in E minor,
'From the New World'   43'

BBC National Orchestra of Wales
Ryan Bancroft *conductor*

There's an American accent to this concert by the
BBC National Orchestra of Wales and its US-born
Principal Conductor Ryan Bancroft. Started just
months after the composer first docked in America,
Dvořák's much-loved 'New World' Symphony was
composed 'in the spirit' of the nation's own songs
and spirituals. Only around 20 years after that,
in 1914, came Charles Ives's *Three Places in New
England*, his vivid musical recollections of the sights
and sounds of his native Connecticut. A topical
new work from American composer Augusta Read
Thomas opens both the concert and our series of
Proms commissions celebrating the Royal Albert
Hall's 150th anniversary and its role in promoting
the arts and sciences. *Dance Foldings* takes inspiration
from the biological 'ballet' of proteins that a vaccine
activates within the human body. *See 'A Gift to the
Nation', pages 36–41.*

Monday 9 August

PROMS AT CADOGAN HALL ②

1.00pm • Cadogan Hall

Josquin des Prez Praeter rerum
seriem   7'

Calvisius Praeter rerum seriem   7'

Josquin des Prez Benedicta es,
caelorum regina   8'

Willaert Benedicta es, caelorum regina   8'

Josquin des Prez Inviolata, integra et
casta es   7'

Lusitano Inviolata, integra et casta es   9'

Marian Consort
Rory McCleery *director*

British vocal ensemble the Marian Consort makes its
Proms debut with a concert celebrating Renaissance
master Josquin des Prez 500 years after his death.
In a season of musical borrowings, three of Josquin's
greatest motets, all drawing on pre-existing material,
are paired with three musical homages — including
the kaleidoscopic *Inviolata, integra et casta es* by the
first published black composer, Vicente Lusitano –
that each rework Josquin's own music for a new age.
*See 'Plunder Enlightening', pages 42–47; 'Renaissance
Resplendence', pages 82–83.*

Monday 9 August

7.30pm • Royal Albert Hall

Mason Bates Auditorium   16'
UK premiere

Elgar Cello Concerto in E minor   30'

Janáček Taras Bulba   23'

Johannes Moser *cello*
Bournemouth Symphony Orchestra
Kirill Karabits *conductor*

The Bournemouth Symphony Orchestra returns
under Chief Conductor Kirill Karabits to recall
memories of music past. In Mason Bates's evocative

**Every Prom live
on BBC Radio 3
and available on
BBC Sounds**

RYAN BANCROFT • 8 AUGUST

JOHN STORGÅRDS • 10 AUGUST

PAVEL KOLESNIKOV • 11 AUGUST

NICHOLAS COLLON • 11 AUGUST

Tuesday 10 August

7.30pm • Royal Albert Hall

Programme to include:

Britta Byström Parallel Universes c9'
BBC commission: world premiere

BBC Philharmonic
John Storgårds *conductor*

Together, the BBC Philharmonic and Chief Guest Conductor John Storgårds have recorded cycles of Finnish and Danish symphonies by Sibelius and Nielsen. Swedish composer Britta Byström's Proms commission for the Royal Albert Hall's 150th anniversary draws on the Swedish-American cosmologist Max Tegmark's notion of a hierarchical multiverse. See 'A Gift to the Nation', pages 36–41.

Wednesday 11 August

7.30pm • Royal Albert Hall

Rachmaninov Rhapsody on a Theme of Paganini 23'
Stravinsky The Firebird – suite (1945) 31'

Tom Service and Nicholas Collon introduce Stravinsky's 'The Firebird' suite c20'

Tom Service *presenter*
Pavel Kolesnikov *piano*

Aurora Orchestra
Nicholas Collon *conductor/presenter*

Nicholas Collon and the Aurora Orchestra's from-memory performances have become a thrilling recent fixture of the Proms. Now, following symphonies by Beethoven, Brahms, Shostakovich

Auditorium, the orchestra is 'possessed' by a ghostly Baroque ancestor; Janáček's rhapsodic suite *Taras Bulba* looks back to Czech folk music in three battle-charged episodes from Gogol's novella. The bittersweet, poignant beauty of Elgar's Cello Concerto draws on another conflict: the cataclysmic loss and suffering of the First World War.

and Berlioz, they tackle their most audacious challenge yet: a complete performance of the colourful 1945 suite from Stravinsky's ballet *The Firebird*. Russian fairy tales and folk melodies collide with Stravinsky's bold musical modernism to create a memorable score. Radio 3 presenter Tom Service introduces the work from the stage, exploring its textures and themes and dismantling its intricate musical narrative with the help of Collon and his musicians. The concert opens with another Russian classic: Rachmaninov's virtuosic *Rhapsody on a Theme of Paganini* for solo piano and orchestra. See 'Plunder Enlightening', pages 42–47; 'Post Progressive', pages 56–60.

These are provisional listings for the 2021 BBC Proms season.

Please note that changes in the Government's Covid-19 regulations may affect programmes, artists, start-times and audience numbers.

Please check the Proms website for the latest information: bbc.co.uk/proms

Spotlight on …

Kirill Karabits • 9 August

Like many conductors, Kirill Karabits faced cancellation after cancellation last year. So, with lockdowns across Europe easing, how does it feel to be back on the podium? 'I have conducted several orchestras recently,' he says, 'but it never feels the same as when I'm in Bournemouth.' It makes sense: he's been Principal Conductor of the Bournemouth Symphony Orchestra since 2009, moulding it into a slick, critically acclaimed ensemble. 'I know the players so well and they are used to my way of communicating. Normally, you have to prove your ideas work – win the musicians over in some way. But I don't have that with the BSO.'

This summer the pair make their seventh joint appearance at the Proms. Karabits has grown used to the unique atmosphere in the Royal Albert Hall, though when he made his debut in 2009 it almost overwhelmed him: 'I don't know how to describe it. When I walked on stage, it felt like a ball of energy, physically hitting me in the face!' Concentrating on the music has become easier with each appearance, but a Prom still requires different mental preparation to other concerts: 'You are building up towards facing that atmosphere. And, because the Proms is always such a celebration of different orchestras, it makes you want to highlight the unique qualities and identity of your ensemble – a moment of truth for us all!'

Thursday 12 August

7.30pm • Royal Albert Hall

Stravinsky Jeu de cartes — 23'
Walton Cello Concerto — 27'
Bach, orch. Goldmann 14 Canons, BWV 1087 (Goldberg Variations) — 17'
Hindemith Symphony 'Mathis der Maler' — 28'

Steven Isserlis cello
London Philharmonic Orchestra
Vladimir Jurowski conductor

Vladimir Jurowski bids farewell to the London Philharmonic Orchestra after nearly 20 years as its Music Director in a concert of the 20th-century repertoire he has championed so passionately during his time in London. The rise of Nazism is the catalyst for both Stravinsky's ballet Jeu de cartes ('Card Game'), in which forces of good triumph over the wicked Joker, and Hindemith's symphony Mathis der Maler ('Mathis the Painter'), in which the demons and angels of the Isenheim Altarpiece are vividly dramatised. Walton's rhapsodic Cello Concerto takes us forwards into the 1950s and the end of the composer's career. Leading British cellist Steven Isserlis is the soloist. See 'Plunder Enlightening', pages 42–47; 'Past Progressive', pages 56–60.

VLADIMIR JUROWSKI • 12 AUGUST

Saturday 14 August

7.30pm • Royal Albert Hall

Prokofiev Symphony No. 1 in D major, 'Classical' — 14'
Bach Keyboard Concerto in F minor, BWV 1056 — 11'
Mozart Piano Concerto No. 24 in C minor, K491 — 31'
Shostakovich Symphony No. 9 in E flat major — 31'

Víkingur Ólafsson piano
Philharmonia Orchestra
Santtu-Matias Rouvali conductor

Award-winning Icelandic pianist Víkingur Ólafsson makes his much-anticipated Proms debut, as soloist in both Bach's Keyboard Concerto in F minor, whose energised outer movements frame a ravishing central Adagio, and Mozart's pioneering Piano Concerto K491, a rare minor-key work whose stormy, richly orchestrated music climaxes in a relentless dance. The Philharmonia Orchestra and its dynamic Finnish Principal Conductor Designate Santtu-Matias Rouvali frame the concert with two symphonies: Prokofiev's playful 'Classical' Symphony, with its clever juxtaposition of traditional forms and contemporary colours, and the more loaded irony of Shostakovich's compact Symphony No. 9. See 'Before I Go on Stage', pages 14–17; 'Plunder Enlightening', pages 42–47.

Proms performances – most recently in 2019, when they delivered 'richly warm and affectionate' accounts of Elgar and Vaughan Williams.

20 Proms on BBC TV and available on BBC iPlayer

Friday 13 August

7.30pm • Royal Albert Hall

Programme to be announced

BBC Symphony Orchestra
Sir Andrew Davis conductor

The BBC Symphony Orchestra is joined by Conductor Laureate Sir Andrew Davis for its second concert of the season. Formerly the orchestra's Chief Conductor, Davis has enjoyed a 30-year relationship with the BBC SO, yielding numerous award-winning recordings as well as memorable

SIR ANDREW DAVIS • 13 AUGUST

VÍKINGUR ÓLAFSSON • 14 AUGUST

SANTTU-MATIAS ROUVALI • 14 AUGUST

Sunday 15 August

7.00pm • Royal Albert Hall

Programme to be announced

Abel Selaocoe cello/voice
Simo Lagnawi guembri
Chesaba
BBC National Orchestra of Wales
Clark Rundell conductor

With 'knock-out charm' to match his virtuoso skill, South African cellist Abel Selaocoe is redefining

These are provisional listings for the 2021 BBC Proms season.

Please note that changes in the Government's Covid-19 regulations may affect programmes, artists, start-times and audience numbers.

Please check the Proms website for the latest information: bbc.co.uk/proms

his instrument and having a blast doing it. Blending traditional playing styles with improvisation, singing and body percussion, his energised performances bring together classical and world music in a unique fusion. He'll be joined by Simo Lagnawi on guembri (three-stringed Moroccan lute) and by other members of his own trio, Chesaba, as well as the BBC National Orchestra of Wales for a concert covering typically broad musical ground.

Monday 16 August

PROMS AT CADOGAN HALL ❸

1.00pm • Cadogan Hall

Haydn String Quartet in D major, Op. 64 No. 5 'Lark'   20'

Simpson String Quartet No. 1   25'

Marmen Quartet

The prize-winning young Marmen Quartet, formed in 2013 at London's Royal College of Music, makes its BBC Proms debut with Haydn's vivacious 'Lark' Quartet, which opens with a soaring violin melody that gives the work its nickname. It is also the inspiration for the String Quartet No. 1 by Robert Simpson, performed in this centenary year of his birth. Its opening draws on Haydn's own initial theme and its ingenious coda reflects Haydn's elegant simplicity, with a nod to Beethoven thrown in for good measure.

Spotlight on …

Abel Selaocoe • 15 August

Abel Selaocoe is not a musician who respects boundaries. In recent years he's redefined the role of solo cellist, incorporating improvisation, singing and body percussion alongside virtuoso performance. In his upcoming Prom he says he wants to find the thread that holds together two parallel worlds: African music and the European Baroque.

What links these apparently unrelated styles? 'There's the improvisational aspect,' he says, 'as well as a rhythmic aspect – we have a culture of repetition in African music which also exists in the Baroque ground bass. I also began looking at colonisation, and influences that ended up coming to places like South Africa, taking inspiration from the old and mixing it with the modern.'

So it's familiar Baroque music but performed with a distinctive personal twist. 'I'll be taking a sonata by Giovanni Benedetto Platti,' explains Selaocoe, 'and using that sonata to speak the same notes but with different voices. I'll be playing the solo part, but we'll also have the ngoni, which is a West African string instrument, and I'll be playing with Simo Lagnawi, who plays the guembri, a Moroccan lute. And we'll be improvising between movements with percussionist Sidiki Dembélé from the Ivory Coast and multi-instrumentalist Alan Keary on bass guitar. This melting pot of music really shows who I am.'

Monday 16 August

7.30pm • Royal Albert Hall

To Soothe the Aching Heart

An evening of opera excerpts on the themes of separation and reconciliation

Sally Matthews *soprano*
Natalya Romaniw *soprano*
Nardus Williams *soprano*
Christine Rice *mezzo-soprano*
Nicky Spence *tenor*
Freddie De Tommaso *tenor*

BBC Philharmonic
Ben Glassberg *conductor*

A host of British opera stars join Ben Glassberg and the BBC Philharmonic for a night rich in emotion and drama. After a year of lockdowns and social distancing, the themes of isolation and loneliness as well as the joy of reunion have particular poignancy in excerpts from much-loved operas including Handel's *Rodelinda*, Beethoven's *Fidelio*, Humperdinck's *Hansel and Gretel* and Puccini's *La bohème*.

Tuesday 17 August

7.30pm • Royal Albert Hall

Górecki Harpsichord Concerto — 9'
Edmund Finnis The Centre is Everywhere — 13'
Eastman The Holy Presence of Joan d'Arc — 21'
Dobrinka Tabakova Suite in Old Style, 'The Court Jester Amareu' — 19'
Joseph Horovitz Jazz Concerto — 15'

Mahan Esfahani *harpsichord*

Manchester Collective
Rakhi Singh *violin/director*

Fresh from the release of its debut recording, the dynamic Manchester Collective makes its first appearance at the Proms with a programme that draws on the musical past to help imagine a bold

musical future. Award-winning harpsichordist Mahan Esfahani explodes stereotypes around his instrument in concertos by Joseph Horovitz and Górecki – the former a witty fusion of jazz colours and textures with Classical forms, the latter a musical 'prank', motoric and defiantly playful. Also looking back to the 18th century is Dobrinka Tabakova's *Suite in Old Style* – a musical homage to Rameau (alias Amareu) that blends folk and Baroque details in its five contrasting movements. The concert also includes music by the black American avant-garde post-Minimalist and gay activist Julius Eastman and Novello Award-nominated composer Edmund Finnis. See *'Plunder Enlightening', pages 42–47.*

These are provisional listings for the 2021 BBC Proms season.

Please note that changes in the Government's Covid-19 regulations may affect programmes, artists, start-times and audience numbers.

Please check the Proms website for the latest information: bbc.co.uk/proms

MAHAN ESFAHANI • 17 AUGUST

SHIVA FESHAREKI • 19 AUGUST

SOFI JEANNIN • 19 AUGUST

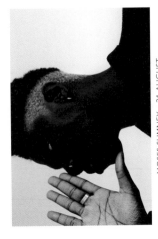

MOSES SUMNEY • 21 AUGUST

Wednesday 18 August

7.30pm • Royal Albert Hall

Nubya Garcia *saxophone*

British saxophonist, composer, DJ and bandleader Nubya Garcia is one of the brightest of a new generation of jazz talent, drawing comparison with greats such as Sonny Rollins and Dexter Gordon. Named a 'major voice' by *The New York Times*, she has devised a brand of 'eclectic, danceable, political jazz' that draws on influences from Africa, Latin America and the Caribbean. Tonight marks her Proms debut.

Thursday 19 August

7.30pm • Royal Albert Hall

Programme to include:

Josquin des Prez Qui habitat in adiutorio altissimi (a 24)   *6'*

Byrd Ave verum corpus   *4'*

Roderick Williams Ave Verum Corpus Re-imagined   *6'*

Stravinsky Otche nash   *2'*

Sweelinck Je sens en moy une flamme nouvelle   *2'*

Nico Muhly A New Flame (after Sweelinck)   *c8'*
BBC commission: world premiere

Shiva Feshareki Aether World   *c12'*
BBC commission: world premiere

Shiva Feshareki *turntables/electronics*
Liam Byrne *viola da gamba*

BBC Singers
Sofi Jeannin *conductor*

Experimental composer and turntablist Shiva Feshareki joins Sofi Jeannin and the BBC Singers for a choral playlist colliding the Renaissance with the present day. Works by Hildegard of Bingen, Byrd and Josquin are woven into a continuous musical sequence with pieces by Stravinsky, Feshareki, Nico Muhly and Roderick Williams. Old and new,

acoustic and electronic, sacred and secular come together in this musical kaleidoscope. *See 'Plunder Enlightening', pages 42–47; 'Past Progressive', pages 56–60; 'Renaissance Resplendence', pages 82–83.*

Friday 20 August

7.30pm • Royal Albert Hall

Please see bbc.co.uk/proms for updates

Saturday 21 August

7.30pm • Royal Albert Hall

Moses Sumney Meets Jules Buckley and the BBC Symphony Orchestra

Moses Sumney

BBC Symphony Orchestra
Jules Buckley *conductor*

Blending soul, jazz, art-pop and spoken word, singer-songwriter Moses Sumney defies traditional categories. His ever-evolving voice has channelled political rage and emotional optimism into everything from sprawling orchestral tracks to electronica. Here he performs songs from his albums *Aromanticism* and *græ* in new orchestral arrangements, masterminded by Jules Buckley. *See 'Ahead of the Curve', pages 78–80.*

Spotlight on …

Nubya Garcia • 18 August

For Nubya Garcia, performing at the Proms feels both natural and surreal. The saxophonist and composer has been coming to the Royal Albert Hall for most of her life: as part of the Camden Schools' Music Festival, Promming up in the Gallery during her teens ('not being able to see much but still feeling part of it') and, most recently, performing with her band in the Women of the World Festival.

'The Proms is going to be a really special part of the journey that I've had in that specific building,' she explains. 'And seeing how the festival has progressed over the years – the involvement of different genres and the movement towards inclusion and diversity – has been a really promising thing to witness. I'm honestly really happy to be a part of that.'

Garcia will be basing much of her set on her critically acclaimed debut album, *Source*, which she calls 'a journey of sonic mantras'. So what's the narrative that binds these songs together? 'It's about personal power, collective power,' she explains. 'Reaching into your identity and groups of identity … It's all basically a deep reflection on where I've come from, where I am and how that sounds musically.' She's hoping it will get the Proms audience moving too: 'My music invites you, or me, or us, to let go of your inhibitions and move. However you move is wherever the music takes you!'

Sunday 22 August

7.30pm • Royal Albert Hall

Stravinsky
Symphonies of Wind Instruments — 12'
Symphony in C — 28'
Symphony in Three Movements — 22'

London Symphony Orchestra
Sir Simon Rattle conductor

The London Symphony Orchestra and Sir Simon Rattle mark 2021's Stravinsky anniversary with a series of symphonic snapshots. We follow Stravinsky's view of the symphony from the experimental, colour-blocked 'ritual' of the *Symphonies of Wind Instruments*, through the transitional *Symphony in C* – reflecting both the composer's European past and his American future – to arrive at the bold *Symphony in Three Movements*. See 'Past Progressive', pages 56–60.

SIR SIMON RATTLE • 22 AUGUST

Monday 23 August

7.30pm • Royal Albert Hall

Please see bbc.co.uk/proms for updates

Tuesday 24 August

7.30pm • Royal Albert Hall

Coleridge-Taylor Hiawatha's Wedding Feast – overture — 5'

Sowande African Suite — 23'

Price Piano Concerto in One Movement — 18'

Coleridge-Taylor Symphony in A minor — 35'

Jeneba Kanneh-Mason piano

Chineke! Orchestra
Kalena Bovell conductor

The Chineke! Orchestra returns for its fourth visit to the Proms, celebrating diversity in composers as well as performers. Black British composer Samuel Coleridge-Taylor's overture to his popular cantata based on the tale of a Native American leader quotes the spiritual 'Nobody knows the trouble I've seen'. There are further meetings of African and European musical styles in Nigerian composer Fela Sowande's *African Suite* and the piano concerto by Florence Price, the first female African-American composer to win renown in America. By contrast, Coleridge-Taylor's Symphony, written as a 20-year-old student of Stanford at London's Royal College of Music, reveals the influence of his hero, Dvořák.

SEAN SHIBE • 23 AUGUST

KALENA BOVELL • 24 AUGUST

ILAN VOLKOV • 26 AUGUST

Monday 23 August

PROMS AT CADOGAN HALL ❹
1.00pm • Cadogan Hall

Programme to include:

Piazzolla Histoire du tango — 20'

Ramírez songs — 20'

Adam Walker flute
Sean Shibe guitars
Singer to be announced

Former BBC Radio 3 New Generation Artist Sean Shibe has been breaking down musical boundaries and winning awards since he erupted onto the classical music scene almost a decade ago. Now the young guitarist makes his much-anticipated Proms debut, joining forces with flautist Adam Walker for a concert celebrating the centenaries of two Argentine composers. Songs by Ariel Ramírez follow Astor Piazzolla's *Histoire du tango* – tracing the dance's colourful history from its origins in the bordellos of Buenos Aires via cafés and nightclubs to the contemporary concert hall.

Wednesday 25 August

7.30pm • Royal Albert Hall

Vivaldi The Four Seasons   37'

interspersed with:

Piazzolla, arr. Desyatnikov   27'
The Four Seasons of Buenos Aires

Academy of St Martin in the Fields
Joshua Bell *violin/director*

From an icy Italian winter to the heady, sensual warmth of a South American summer: violinist Joshua Bell leads the Academy of St Martin in the Fields on a musical journey through the sights and sounds of two continents and four very different seasons. Inspired by Vivaldi's best-known work, Piazzolla – Argentina's 20th-century tango king, whose 100th anniversary we celebrate this year – created his own response, complete with musical quotations. While Vivaldi's virtuosic concertos celebrate contrast – the freshness of spring, with its sudden thunderstorms, versus the languid heat of summer – Piazzolla's musical landscape remains more constant, always swaying to the pervasive rhythm of the tango. *See 'Plunder Enlightening', pages 42–47.*

These are provisional listings for the 2021 BBC Proms season.

Please note that changes in the Government's Covid-19 regulations may affect programmes, artists, start-times and audience numbers.

Please check the Proms website for the latest information: bbc.co.uk/proms

---

Thursday 26 August

7.30pm • Royal Albert Hall

George Lewis Minds in Flux   c30'
BBC commission: world premiere

Beethoven
Concert aria 'Ah! perfido'   13'
Symphony No. 2 in D major   32'

Lucy Crowe *soprano*
BBC Scottish Symphony Orchestra
Ilan Volkov *conductor*

The BBC Scottish Symphony Orchestra and Principal Guest Conductor Ilan Volkov pair Beethoven's dramatic concert aria 'Ah! perfido' with the Second Symphony – a work whose vitality and 'smiling' mood belie the private struggles and despair of a composer wrestling with hearing loss – with a new commission from celebrated American composer George Lewis. This world premiere blends a conventional orchestra with spatialised electronics, exploiting the unique space of the Royal Albert Hall to create, in Lewis's words, 'a medium for meditation on what processes of decolonisation might sound like.'

Spotlight on …

Joshua Bell • 25 August

Indiana-born Joshua Bell has been Music Director of London's Academy of St Martin in the Fields for a decade now. For his 21st appearance at the Proms, though, he's revelling in a rather different sort of European–American exchange. 'They're two wildly different works,' he says of the Four Seasons of Antonio Vivaldi and Astor Piazzolla, 'and yet there is a common thread between them, as well as great contrast.'

There may be a world of difference between Vivaldi's depictions of rural Mediterranean scenes and Piazzolla's menacing Argentine cityscapes but the two works illuminate each other when alternated in sequence. 'Vivaldi was ahead of his time in exploiting the colours of the orchestra, and even sound effects,' explains Bell. 'And Piazzolla was the master at mixing tango, jazz and classical genres to create amazing colours. The unique atmosphere of the Proms will be just right for this celebration of music.'

Piazzolla performed his Four Seasons of Buenos Aires with his own band, leading from the accordion-like bandoneón. How does that translate to the milieu of the chamber orchestra? 'Vivaldi was a violinist and wrote his concertos as virtuoso showpieces,' says Bell, 'and that's exactly what Russian composer Leonid Desyatnikov has done to Piazzolla's bandoneón originals, working with violinist Gidon Kremer to create a vehicle that really shows off the instrument in wonderful ways.'

Friday 27 August

7.30pm • Royal Albert Hall

Programme to include:

Charlotte Bray Where Icebergs
Dance Away
UK premiere

Walton Viola Concerto

Arnold Symphony No. 5

BBC Symphony Orchestra
Sakari Oramo *conductor*
Soloist to be announced

A world away from centenary composer Malcolm Arnold's reputation for light music and film scores (see 2 September), the Fifth Symphony is a richly layered work full of irony, pain and loss. An opening musical 'garden of memories' pays affectionate homage to departed friends, while the scherzo flirts with jazz and the finale offers a tantalising glimpse of heaven before snatching it cruelly away. Walton's poetic Viola Concerto was given its world premiere at the Proms in 1929. Global warming is the stimulus behind Charlotte Bray's *Where Icebergs Dance Away*, which draws on the work of American artist Zaria Forman. *See 'Before I Go on Stage', pages 14–17.*

SAKARI ORAMO • 27 AUGUST

The BBC Scottish Symphony Orchestra and Chief Conductor Thomas Dausgaard explore the rough-hewn rhythms and the lyrical melodies that unite Bartók's Violin Concerto with the Magyar music that so fascinated the composer. *See 'Before I Go on Stage', pages 14–17; 'Plunder Enlightening', pages 42–47.*

Sunday 29 August

7.00pm • Royal Albert Hall

Family Prom

Programme to include:

Saint-Saëns The Carnival of
the Animals
with new narration by Michael Morpurgo 39'

Aminata Kanneh-Mason *violin*
Braimah Kanneh-Mason *violin*
Ayla Sahin *violin*
Timothy Ridout *viola*
Mariatu Kanneh-Mason *cello*
Sheku Kanneh-Mason *cello*
Toby Hughes *double bass*
Adam Walker *flute*
Mark Simpson *clarinet*
Isata Kanneh-Mason *piano*
Jeneba Kanneh-Mason *piano*
Konya Kanneh-Mason *piano*
Alasdair Malloy *glass harmonica*
Adrian Spillett *percussion*
Michael Morpurgo *narrator*

British Sign Language-interpreted performance

MICHAEL MORPURGO • 29 AUGUST

Author Michael Morpurgo joins the seven talented Kanneh-Mason siblings and starry musical friends for this special Family Prom. Saint-Saëns's much-loved suite *The Carnival of the Animals* – a musical menagerie packed with braying donkeys, energetic kangaroos, a serene swan and an aquarium of glinting fish – gets a fresh update in witty new poems by Morpurgo. *See 'A Family Affair', pages 62–64.*

Saturday 28 August

7.30pm • Royal Albert Hall

Bartók Roots

Programme to include:

Bartók Violin Concerto No. 2 36'

Patricia Kopatchinskaja *violin*

BBC Scottish Symphony Orchestra
Thomas Dausgaard *conductor*

In a memorable Prom in 2019, violinist Pekka Kuusisto took Sibelius's Violin Concerto back to its roots in Finnish folk music. Now the dazzling, fearless Patricia Kopatchinskaja takes up the challenge, tracing the same evolution from traditional Hungarian songs and dances to Bartók's Violin Concerto No. 2.

FRANÇOIS LELEUX • 30 AUGUST

SIR GEORGE BENJAMIN • 30 AUGUST

Monday 30 August

1.00pm • Cadogan Hall

Saint-Saëns Oboe Sonata — 11'

Gipps Sea-Shore Suite — 6'

Dutilleux Oboe Sonata — 10'

Poulenc Oboe Sonata — 11'

Bozza Fantaisie pastorale — 6'

François Leleux *oboe*
Eric Le Sage *piano*

A triptych of 20th-century sonatas by Saint-Saëns, Dutilleux and Poulenc forms the heart of this all-French programme. The cool lines of Saint-Saëns's neo-Classical sonata give way to the edgier, mercurial beauty of Dutilleux's, while the Poulenc pays musical homage to its dedicatee, Sergey Prokofiev, ending with a ravishing lament. Eugène Bozza's lyrical *Fantaisie pastorale* and Ruth Gipps's vivid *Sea-Shore Suite* complete the recital. See 'An Indomitable Maverick', pages 52–54.

Monday 30 August

7.30pm • Royal Albert Hall

Knussen The Way to Castle Yonder — 8'

Purcell, orch. Benjamin Fantasias — c11'
world premiere

Ravel Piano Concerto in G major — 23'

George Benjamin Concerto for Orchestra — c18'
world premiere

Pierre-Laurent Aimard *piano*
Mahler Chamber Orchestra
Sir George Benjamin *conductor*

BBC co-commission with Mahler Chamber Orchestra: world premiere

When the 20-year-old George Benjamin's *Ringed by the Flat Horizon* was performed at the Proms in 1980, it marked an arrival for a precociously talented young composer. Now established as one of the greats of

his generation, he returns to conduct regular collaborators, the Mahler Chamber Orchestra and pianist Pierre-Laurent Aimard, in a concert featuring Ravel's jazz-infused Piano Concerto, an operatic 'pot-pourri' by his friend, the late Oliver Knussen, the world premiere of his own *Concerto for Orchestra* and his new reworkings of Fantasias by Purcell, the 'English Orpheus'. See 'Plunder Enlightening', pages 42–47.

These are provisional listings for the 2021 BBC Proms season.

Please note that changes in the Government's Covid-19 regulations may affect programmes, artists, start-times and audience numbers.

Please check the Proms website for the latest information:
bbc.co.uk/proms

Spotlight on …

Patricia Kopatchinskaja • 28 August

With a musical appetite that is strikingly voracious and wide-ranging, Patricia Kopatchinskaja is a musical force of nature who challenges convention. But her Prom with the BBC Scottish Symphony Orchestra, exploring the folk roots of Bartók's music, represents a personal journey that reminds her of home.

Born in Soviet-ruled Moldova, Kopatchinskaja grew up close to her country's folk culture. 'Bartók collected folk music not only from his native Hungary', she explains, 'but also from Romania and Moldova. His Second Violin Concerto feels like my lost homeland, the fairy tales I heard from my grandmother, even the singing of the priests in the Orthodox churches, the cimbalom played by angels in my dreams as a child, the black earth. I cannot relate to any other concerto in this way.'

Now resident in Switzerland, having studied in Vienna, Kopatchinskaja first came into contact with the concerto around 20 years ago, and it was a baptism of fire. 'I had to learn it in a week. It felt like the battle of a mortal against a three-headed, fire-breathing dragon. Inhumanly difficult.'

How will the work play out in the Royal Albert Hall? 'In such a large venue one needs a special energy to embrace the whole space, like a lamp: the spirit has to burn brighter to illuminate all corners.'

Tuesday 31 August

4.00pm • Royal Albert Hall

Wagner Tristan and Isolde
(concert performance; sung in German)

Simon O'Neill *Tristan*
Miina-Liisa Värelä *Isolde*
Karen Cargill *Brangäne*
Shenyang *Kurwenal*
John Relyea *King Mark*
Neal Cooper *Melot*
Stuart Jackson *Shepherd/Young Sailor*

Glyndebourne Festival Opera
London Philharmonic Orchestra
Robin Ticciati *conductor*

'I am still looking for a work with as dangerous a fascination, with as terrible and sweet an infinity as *Tristan*,' Nietzsche wrote of Wagner's great love-tragedy. A story about longing and yearning, about an unresolved and unresolvable love, expressed in music that famously denies us resolution until its very final bars, the opera still exerts the same fascination today. Glyndebourne Music Director Robin Ticciati conducts an international cast in a concert performance marking 60 years of the company's performances at the Proms.

Wednesday 1 September

7.30pm • Royal Albert Hall

Handel Donna, che in ciel   30'
Bach Christ lag in Todes Banden, BWV 4   22'
Handel Dixit Dominus   31'

Ann Hallenberg *mezzo-soprano*

Monteverdi Choir
English Baroque Soloists
Sir John Eliot Gardiner *conductor*

Sir John Eliot Gardiner makes his 60th Proms appearance directing his own Monteverdi Choir and English Baroque Soloists in Handel's vividly theatrical *Dixit Dominus* – a concerto for choir that blazes with virtuosity and colour. It's paired with Bach's Easter cantata *Christ lag in Todes Banden* – a fiery, dramatic setting of Luther's popular hymn. Mezzo-soprano Ann Hallenberg is the soloist in the young Handel's cantata of praise to the Virgin Mary, *Donna, che in ciel*, containing music the composer later borrowed for his opera *Agrippina*. See '*Plunder Enlightening*', pages 42–47.

Thursday 2 September

7.30pm • Royal Albert Hall

20th-Century British Film Music

Classic soundtracks by composers including Malcolm Arnold, Ralph Vaughan Williams and Doreen Carwithen

BBC Concert Orchestra
Bramwell Tovey *conductor*

English composers of the 20th century could rival their counterparts across the Atlantic when it came to creating some of the most memorable cinematic moments of the century. Spend a night at the movies with a sequence of classic British film scores, brought to life by the BBC Concert Orchestra and Principal Conductor Bramwell Tovey.

20 Proms on BBC TV and available on BBC iPlayer

ROBIN TICCIATI • 31 AUGUST

ANN HALLENBERG • 1 SEPTEMBER

KIRILL GERSTEIN • 3 SEPTEMBER

MIAH PERSSON • 4 SEPTEMBER

Friday 3 September

7.30pm • Royal Albert Hall

Programme to be announced

Kirill Gerstein *piano*

BBC Symphony Orchestra
Semyon Bychkov *conductor*

Russian-American pianist Kirill Gerstein returns to the Proms following his thrilling 2017 performance of Rachmaninov's First Piano Concerto, rekindling his partnership with the BBC Symphony Orchestra and the holder of the orchestra's Günter Wand Conducting Chair, Semyon Bychkov.

These are provisional listings for the 2021 BBC Proms season.

Please note that changes in the Government's Covid-19 regulations may affect programmes, artists, start-times and audience numbers.

Please check the Proms website for the latest information:
bbc.co.uk/proms

Saturday 4 September

matinee • Royal Albert Hall

Organ Recital

Programme to include:

Thomas Trotter *organ*

Saint-Saëns Fantaisie in E flat major   6'
Liszt Fantasy and Fugue on 'Ad nos, ad salutarem undam'   30'

One of the world's leading organists, Thomas Trotter pays tribute to centenary composer Saint-Saëns in a programme that recreates elements of the composer's legendary performances on the Royal Albert Hall organ in the opening season of 1871 and in 1880. *See 'A Gift to the Nation', pages 36–41.*

Saturday 4 September

7.30pm • Royal Albert Hall

J. Strauss II Die Fledermaus – overture   8'
Berg Seven Early Songs   18'
Ravel La valse   12'
Korngold Symphony in F sharp major   50'

Miah Persson *soprano*
Sinfonia of London
John Wilson *conductor*

The award-winning Sinfonia of London makes its much-anticipated official concert debut under John Wilson, who re-established the ensemble in 2018. Following on from their award-winning recording, this orchestral 'army of generals' brings with it Korngold's stirring, filmic Symphony in F sharp major. It's part of a musical bird's-eye view of 19th- and 20th-century Vienna that also includes the overture to Die Fledermaus and Ravel's dizzying La valse.

Spotlight on …

John Wilson • 4 September

When conductor John Wilson relaunched the Sinfonia of London in 2018, the idea was simply to record a disc featuring Erich Wolfgang Korngold's Symphony in F sharp major – which he brings to the Proms with his new orchestra.

Written on the composer's return to Vienna after more than a decade writing film scores in Hollywood, the symphony is a technicoloured showcase and a hymn to 'expression, beauty, melody' – qualities that Korngold held dear even into the 1950s.

In the spirit of the Sinfonia of London's origins as an agile freelance band formed in 1955, Wilson assembled a crack team of musicians. 'But what I wasn't prepared for was just how thrilling the playing would be and how quickly we established a rapport,' he relishes the intimacy of the Royal Albert Hall. 'You can really hear each other and you feel completely connected. Plus, just think of everyone who's played there … There's music seeping out of those walls.'

That one-off recording project has become an eight-disc series, of which five have already been issued, and two – the Korngold disc and Respighi's 'Roman trilogy' – have won *BBC Music Magazine* Awards. Now the orchestra is making its official concert debut and, says Wilson, 'There was only one place I wanted that to be.'

The Proms is where Wilson has enjoyed 'some of my greatest musical thrills'. And

These are provisional listings for the 2021 BBC Proms season.

Please note that changes in the Government's Covid-19 regulations may affect programmes, artists, start-times and audience numbers.

Please check the Proms website for the latest information: bbc.co.uk/proms

Sunday 5 September

7.30pm • Royal Albert Hall

Dvořák Cello Concerto in B minor   40'

Grace-Evangeline Mason   c12'
The Imagined Forest
BBC co-commission with Royal Liverpool Philharmonic Orchestra: world premiere

R. Strauss Don Juan   17'

Hindemith Symphonic Metamorphosis   40'
of Themes by Carl Maria von Weber

Sheku Kanneh-Mason *cello*

Royal Liverpool Philharmonic Orchestra
Domingo Hindoyan *conductor*

Following his Family Prom alongside siblings and friends (see 29 August), former BBC Young Musician winner Sheku Kanneh-Mason returns as the soloist in Dvořák's Cello Concerto. A new Proms commission written for the Royal Albert Hall's 150th anniversary by former BBC Young Composer winner Grace-Evangeline Mason contrasts with two scintillating orchestral showpieces – Hindemith's jovial reworking of themes by Weber for what was initially intended as a ballet, and Richard Strauss's colourful take on the Spanish lothario Don Juan. The Royal Liverpool Philharmonic Orchestra makes its first Proms appearance under its new Chief Conductor, Domingo Hindoyan. See *'Plunder Enlightening', pages 42–47; 'Tomorrow's Voices', pages 66–68.*

Monday 6 September

PROMS AT CADOGAN HALL ❻
1.00pm • Cadogan Hall

Pauline Viardot and Her Circle

Ema Nikolovska *mezzo-soprano*
Malcolm Martineau *piano*

A household name across Europe during the late 19th century, Pauline Viardot was an international opera star by 18, studied the piano with Liszt, played duets with Chopin, charmed Saint-Saëns, Berlioz,

Gounod and the writer Turgenev, and hosted the greatest musical salon of her day. She was also a fine composer, though one still heard too rarely today. BBC New Generation Artist Ema Nikolovska and pianist Malcolm Martineau invite you to step into Viardot's drawing room for a lunchtime recital of music by Viardot, her friends and her contemporaries – including Gounod, Brahms, Tchaikovsky and Chopin. See *'Musician, Muse, Motivator', pages 26–28.*

EMA NIKOLOVSKA • 6 SEPTEMBER

ANNA-MARIA HELSING • 6 SEPTEMBER

SIR MARK ELDER • 7 SEPTEMBER

STUART SKELTON • 11 SEPTEMBER

Monday 6 September

7.30pm • Royal Albert Hall

Philip Glass Mad Rush 11′

Samy Moussa A Globe Itself
Infolding
UK premiere

James McVinnie *organ*

BBC Concert Orchestra
Anna-Maria Helsing *conductor*

James McVinnie is a chameleon among organists who has held titles at Westminster Abbey and St Paul's Cathedral, yet also worked with Philip Glass and The National's Bryce Dessner. In a Prom that explores the organ in a contemporary light, he navigates the time-warping oscillations of Philip Glass's Minimalist *Mad Rush*, before giving the UK premiere of Canadian composer Samy Moussa's *A Globe Itself Infolding* with the Concert Orchestra and Principal Guest Conductor Anna-Maria Helsing. *See 'A Gift to the Nation', pages 36–41.*

Tuesday 7 September

7.30pm • Royal Albert Hall

Unsuk Chin Subito con forza 5′
BBC co-commission: UK premiere

Beethoven Piano Concerto No. 4 34′
in G major *(cadenzas: Saint-Saëns)*

Saint-Saëns Symphony No. 3 36′
in C minor, 'Organ'

Benjamin Grosvenor *piano*
Anna Lapwood *organ*

Hallé
Sir Mark Elder *conductor*

'What I have here accomplished, I will never achieve again.' So wrote Camille Saint-Saëns of his last – and greatest – symphony, a work full of melody, invention and sonic drama (not to mention a piano-duet effect he liked so much he recycled it in

The Carnival of the Animals). Just as the mighty 'Organ' Symphony rewrote the 19th-century musical rules, so Beethoven's Piano Concerto No. 4 scandalised audiences some 80 years earlier, with its revolutionary opening and tender, slow-movement battle between soloist and orchestra – famously compared to Orpheus taming the Furies. Beethoven is also the inspiration for Unsuk Chin's volatile *Subito con forza,* given its UK premiere here by Sir Mark Elder and the Hallé. *See 'Plunder Enlightening', pages 42–47.*

Wednesday 8 September

7.30pm • Royal Albert Hall

Please see bbc.co.uk/proms for updates

Thursday 9 September

7.00pm • Royal Albert Hall

Bach St Matthew Passion 180′
(sung in German)

Soloists to include:

Stuart Jackson *Evangelist*
Hugo Hymas *tenor*
Roderick Williams *baritone*
Gerald Finley *Jesus*

Arcangelo Chorus
Arcangelo
Jonathan Cohen *harpsichord/director*

Bach's crowning masterpiece, the *St Matthew Passion* combines moments of extraordinary fragility and tenderness with raw choral power, bitter grief with passages of consolation and explosive jubilation. With double chorus and orchestra, its scope and ambition is vast – a piece made for the Royal Albert Hall. Following on from their gripping account of Handel's *Theodora* in 2018, period-instrument ensemble Arcangelo and Director Jonathan Cohen return to the Proms, joined by a glittering line-up of soloists including Gerald Finley and Roderick Williams.

Friday 10 September

7.30pm • Royal Albert Hall

Please see bbc.co.uk/proms for updates

Saturday 11 September

7.30pm • Royal Albert Hall

Last Night of the Proms 2021

Programme to include:

arr. Wood Fantasia on British 17′
Sea-Songs

Arne, arr. Sargent Rule, Britannia! 4′

Elgar Pomp and Circumstance 8′
March No. 1 in D major ('Land of
Hope and Glory')

Parry, orch. Elgar Jerusalem 2′

arr. Britten The National Anthem 3′
Trad. Auld Lang Syne

Stuart Skelton *tenor*
Ksenija Sidorova *accordion*

BBC Singers
BBC Symphony Orchestra
Sakari Oramo *conductor*

With his 'thrilling vocal heroics' and 'magnetic stage presence', Stuart Skelton is one of the great tenors of his generation, a regular in all the major international opera houses. The Australian singer is joined by charismatic Latvian accordionist Ksenija Sidorova for the climax of the 2021 festival – a musical celebration like no other. *See 'Before I Go on Stage', pages 14–17; 'There once was a ship that put to sea . . .', pages 84–86.*

BBC singers

BBC Philharmonic

BBC National Orchestra of Wales / Cerddorfa Genedlaethol Gymreig y BBC

BBC Concert Orchestra

ORCHESTRAS & CHOIRS

MUSIC FOR EVERYONE

FROM THE HEART

BBC SOUNDS

BBC iPlayer

BBC.CO.UK/ORCHESTRAS

BBC Symphony Orchestra & Chorus

BBC Scottish Symphony Orchestra

Booking

Booking Period 1

21 June
Create your
Proms Plan online

From Monday 21 June, you can go to bbc.co.uk/proms and fill in your Proms Plan for all concerts taking place between 30 July and 20 August. You must complete your Plan by 11.59pm on Friday 25 June in order to make a booking with it. Creating a Plan does not by itself result in a booking.

26 June
General Booking Opens

From 9.00am on Saturday 26 June booking opens for all concerts taking place between 30 July and 20 August. Submit your Proms Plan or book online via bbc.co.uk/proms or by phone. See bbc.co.uk/promstickets for details of how to book.

Booking Period 2

10 July
Create your
Proms Plan online

From Saturday 10 July, you can go to bbc.co.uk/proms and fill in your Proms Plan for all concerts taking place between 21 August and 10 September (see overleaf for Last Night details). You must complete your Plan by 11.59pm on Friday 16 July in order to make a booking with it. Creating a Plan does not by itself result in a booking.

17 July
General Booking Opens

From 9.00am on Saturday 17 July booking opens for all concerts taking place between 21 August and 10 September, as well as for earlier concerts if they are available (see overleaf for Last Night details). Submit your Proms Plan or book online via bbc.co.uk/proms or by phone. See bbc.co.uk/promstickets for details of how to book.

Online

bbc.co.uk/proms or
royalalberthall.com

By phone

on 020 7070 4441
(from 9.00am on 26 June)†

As a result of Covid-19 safety measures, advance booking in person at the Royal Albert Hall or by post will not be available. Please check the Hall's website for updates.

Royal Albert Hall Ticket Prices

Seated tickets for all concerts at the Royal Albert Hall are placed into price bands, starting at £7.50. See bbc.co.uk/promstickets for details.

A booking fee of 2% of the total value – plus £2.00 per ticket up to a maximum of £25.00 – applies to all bookings made online or by phone.

Promming tickets are available on the day only. For Promming information, see overleaf.

Covid-19

We are hoping to welcome the maximum number of audience members that are safely allowed and will be following Government guidance. For the latest distancing measures, and details of how you can safely enjoy your Proms visit, go to bbc.co.uk/promstickets.

Please also check the latest programme updates at bbc.co.uk/proms before you book or attend.

---

† CALL COSTS
Standard geographic charges from landlines and mobiles apply. All calls may be recorded and monitored for training and quality-control purposes.

Covid-19

We ask you not to attend concerts if, in the 10 days before a performance, you have symptoms of Covid-19 (high temperature, a new, continuous cough, or a loss or change to your sense of taste or smell), or have tested positive for Covid-19, or have come into close contact with anyone who has symptoms of Covid-19 or has tested positive for Covid-19. To confirm your non-attendance, please contact the Royal Albert Hall by 9.00am on the day of the performance, either by calling the 020 7070 4441 or by filling in the online refund form at royalalberthall.com.

Refunds

If you have symptoms, or if you are unable to travel owing to Covid-19 restrictions, please see royalalberthall.com or phone the Box Office on 020 7070 4441 for the latest information on refunds. Refunds are available if a performance is cancelled.

Promming

The popular tradition of Promming (standing in the Arena or Gallery areas of the Royal Albert Hall) is central to the unique and informal atmosphere of the Proms. It is also one of the most difficult things to manage at this time. We therefore ask you to visit bbc.co.uk/proms closer to the season for confirmation of whether Prommers will be able to stand. Should Promming not be possible, seated tickets honouring the ethos of Promming (accessibly priced and available on the day) will be purchasable, although these may not be located in the Arena or Gallery. Promming tickets are £7.12 (including £1.12 booking fee) and are available to buy, online only, on the day of the concert. See bbc.co.uk/promstickets for details.

Promming Passes

Owing to exceptional production requirements, the capacity of the Arena and Gallery will be reduced this season. As a result, we are not able to offer Promming Passes this year.

Online booking

The 'Select Your Own Seat' option is not available via the Proms Planner or during the first few days that Proms tickets are on sale. You will be allocated the best available seats within your chosen seating area. The option will not be available if social-distancing measures are in place.

Allocation of boxes is dependent on whether performances will be socially distanced. Please see royalalberthall.com for the most up-to-date information.

General availability for the Last Night

Any tickets remaining after the ballots will go on sale at 9.00am on **Friday 13 August** by phone or online only. Only one application (for a maximum of two tickets) can be made per household. There is exceptionally high demand for Last Night tickets, but returns occasionally become available.

Promming at the Last Night

Should Promming go ahead this season, a limited number of Promming tickets will be available, online only, on the Last Night itself (priced £7.12, including £1.12 booking fee). See bbc.co.uk/promstickets for details.

Access at the Proms

ACCESS INFORMATION LINE
020 7070 4410 (9.00am–9.00pm daily).

Full information on the exact facilities offered to disabled concert-goers at the Royal Albert Hall will be available closer to the start of the season online at royalalberthall.com or by calling the Access Information Line.

The Royal Albert Hall has a Silver award from the Attitude is Everything Charter of Best Practice.

All disabled concert-goers (and one companion) receive a 50% discount on all ticket prices for all Proms concerts (except for Arena and Gallery areas of the Royal Albert Hall). Book online at bbc.co.uk/proms or, if you need a transfer wheelchair or have specific access requirements, by calling the Access Information Line.

A number of spaces are bookable for wheelchair-users with adjacent companion

18s and under go half-price

Tickets for people aged 18 and under can be purchased at half-price in any seating area for all Proms except the Last Night. (Not applicable to £7.12 Promming tickets.)

Group bookings

Availability of group bookings is dependent on whether performances will be socially distanced. Please see royalalberthall.com for the most up-to-date information on group bookings.

Proms at ... Cadogan Hall

Stalls: £16.00, Centre Gallery: £13.00 (booking fees apply). Cadogan Hall Promming tickets will be sold online. Cadogan Hall Promming Passes are not available this year. See bbc.co.uk/promstickets for details.

Last Night of the Proms

Owing to high demand, the majority of seated tickets for the Last Night of the Proms are allocated via ballots. See bbc.co.uk/promstickets for details.

Visit bbc.co.uk/promstickets for full details of how to book, booking fees and terms and conditions

The Cadogan Hall concert hall opened in June 2004. It is home to the Royal Philharmonic Orchestra and has hosted the BBC Proms Monday-lunchtime chamber music series since 2005.

Cadogan Hall

5 Sloane Terrace, London SW1X 9DQ
www.cadoganhall.com • 020 7730 4500

BBC Proms Festival Guide –
Braille and large-print formats

Braille versions of this Festival Guide are available in two parts, 'Articles' and 'Concert Listings/Booking Information', priced £4.00 each. For more information and to order, call the RNIB Helpline on 0303 123 9999.

A text-only large-print version of this Festival Guide is available, priced £8.00.

To order, call Deborah Fether on 07716 225658, or email promspublications@bbc.co.uk. (Allow 10 working days for delivery.)

The Guide is also available to purchase as an eBook and in ePDF format. Both are compatible with screen readers and text-to-speech software. Visit bbc.co.uk/proms for details.

seats for the whole of the Proms season at the Royal Albert Hall. To book, call the Access Information Line.

Dress code

Come as you are; there is no dress code at the Proms.

Children under 5

Everyone is welcome at the Family Prom (29 August). Out of consideration for artists and audiences, we recommend that children attending other Proms are aged 5 and over.

Security

Please do not bring large bags to the Royal Albert Hall. All bags and visitors will be subject to security checks as a condition of entry.

Latecomers

Latecomers will only be admitted if and when there is a suitable break in the performance.

The Royal Albert Hall has been home to the Proms since 1941, hosting over 4,500 Proms concerts in that time. Officially opened by Queen Victoria on 29 March 1871, this year the Hall celebrates its 150th anniversary.

Royal Albert Hall

Kensington Gore, London SW7 2AP
www.royalalberthall.com • 020 7070 4441

The nearest London Underground station is Sloane Square (Circle & District Lines). There is a bar on site and the venue is wheelchair-accessible.

Proms programmes

For information on how to purchase Proms programmes, see royalalberthall.com.

Travel

The nearest London Underground stations are South Kensington (Circle & District Lines – closed to Piccadilly Line trains until spring 2022), Gloucester Road (Piccadilly, Circle & District Lines) and High Street Kensington (Circle & District Lines).
Additional closures are planned at South Kensington station throughout the year. Please check before you travel at tfl.gov.uk.

A limited number of parking spaces, priced £10.75 each, are available from one hour before the concerts in the Imperial College car park. They can be purchased through the Royal Albert Hall website or by calling 020 7070 4441.

Food and drink

Audience members should not bring their own food and drink into the Hall. Instead, it can be purchased from the Hall from two and a half hours before each concert – see royalalberthall.com for details.

Cloakroom

If the Hall is operating at full capacity and Government guidelines permit it, a cloakroom will be available – a charge of £1.00 per item will apply. Cloakroom season tickets, priced £20.40, will also be available (conditions apply – see royalalberthall.com for details).

Once you have booked tickets, look out for email updates with the latest visitor information

Index of Artists

P@CH indicates 'Proms at … Cadogan Hall' chamber music concerts

first appearance at a BBC Henry Wood Promenade Concert
†current / ‡former member of BBC Radio 3's New Generation Artists scheme

— A

Pierre-Laurent Aimard *piano* 30 Aug

— B

Richard Balcombe *conductor* 31 Jul
Ryan Bancroft *conductor* 8 Aug
Joshua Bell *violin/director* 25 Aug
Nicola Benedetti *violin* 7 Aug
Sir George Benjamin *conductor* 30 Aug
Kalena Bovell* *conductor* 24 Aug
Adrian Brendel* *cello* P@CH 1
Jules Buckley *conductor* 21 Aug
Semyon Bychkov *conductor* 3 Sep
Liam Byrne* *viola da gamba* 19 Aug

— C

Karen Cargill *mezzo-soprano* 31 Aug
Joana Carneiro* *conductor* 6 Aug
Elim Chan *conductor* 2 Aug
Jonathan Cohen *harpsichord/director* 9 Sep
Michael Collins *clarinet* P@CH 1
Nicholas Colton *conductor/presenter* 11 Aug
Neal Cooper* *tenor* 31 Aug
Lucy Crowe *soprano* 26 Aug

— D

Eli Danker* *actor* 3 Aug
Thomas Dausgaard *conductor* 28 Aug
Sir Andrew Davis *conductor* 13 Aug
Freddie De Tommaso* *tenor* 16 Aug

— E

Sir Mark Elder *conductor* 7 Sep
Maxim Emelyanychev *conductor* 1 Aug
Mahan Esfahani‡ *harpsichord* 17 Aug

— F

Shiva Feshareki *turntables* 19 Aug
Gerald Finley *bass-baritone* 9 Sep

— G

Nubya Garcia* *saxophone* 18 Aug
Sir John Eliot Gardiner *conductor* 1 Sep
Kirill Gerstein *piano* 3 Sep
Ben Glassberg* *conductor* 16 Aug
Mirga Gražinytė-Tyla *conductor* 5 Aug
Benjamin Grosvenor‡ *piano* 7 Sep

— H

Ann Hallenberg *mezzo-soprano* 1 Sep
Anna-Maria Helsing* *conductor* 6 Sep
Jonathon Heyward* *conductor* 7 Aug
Domingo Hindoyan* *conductor* 5 Sep
Toby Hughes* *double bass* 29 Aug
Benjamin Hulett *tenor* 6 Aug
Daniel Hyde *organ* 30 Jul
Hugo Hymas* *tenor* 9 Sep

— I

Steven Isserlis *cello* 12 Aug

— J

Stuart Jackson* *tenor* 31 Aug, 9 Sep
Sophie Jeannin *conductor* 19 Aug
Vladimir Jurowski *conductor* 12 Aug

— K

Aminata Kanneh-Mason* *violin* 29 Aug
Braimah Kanneh-Mason* *violin* 29 Aug
Isata Kanneh-Mason *piano* 29 Aug
Jeneba Kanneh-Mason* *piano* 24, 29 Aug
Konya Kanneh-Mason* *piano* 29 Aug
Mariatu Kanneh-Mason* *cello* 29 Aug
Sheku Kanneh-Mason *cello* 29 Aug, 5 Sep
Kirill Karabits *conductor* 9 Aug
Pavel Kolesnikov† *piano* 11 Aug
Patricia Kopatchinskaja* *violin* 28 Aug

— L

Simo Lagnawi* *guembri* 15 Aug
Anna Lapwood* *organ* 7 Sep
François Leleux *oboe* P@CH 5
Eric Le Sage *piano* P@CH 5

— M

Rory McCleery* *director* P@CH 2
Michael McHale* *piano* P@CH 1
James McVinnie* *organ* 6 Sep
Alasdair Malloy *glass harmonica* 29 Aug
Malcolm Martineau *piano* P@CH 6
Sally Matthews‡ *soprano* 16 Aug
Tim Mead *counter-tenor* 6 Aug
Johannes Moser *cello* 9 Aug
Michael Morpurgo* *narrator* 29 Aug

— N

Ema Nikolovska*† *mezzo-soprano* P@CH 6

— O

Víkingur Ólafsson* *piano* 14 Aug
Simon O'Neill *tenor* 31 Aug
Sakari Oramo *conductor* 27 Aug,11 Sep

—P

Miah Persson soprano 4 Sep
Vasily Petrenko conductor 4 Aug

—R

Sir Simon Rattle conductor 22 Aug
John Relyea bass-baritone 31 Aug
Christine Rice† mezzo-soprano 16 Aug
Timothy Ridout*† viola 29 Aug
Natalya Romaniw soprano 16 Aug
Santtu-Matias Rouvali* conductor 14 Aug
Clark Rundell conductor 15 Aug

—S

Ayla Sahin* violin 29 Aug
Carolyn Sampson soprano 6 Aug
Abel Selaocoe* cello/voice 15 Aug
Tom Service presenter 11 Aug
Shenyang* bass-baritone 31 Aug
Simon Shibambu* bass-baritone 6 Aug
Sean Shibe*‡ guitars P@CH 4
Sayaka Shoji* violin 4 Aug
Ksenija Sidorova* accordion 11 Sep
Mark Simpson clarinet 29 Aug
Rakhi Singh* violin/director 17 Aug
Stuart Skelton tenor 11 Sep
Nicky Spence tenor 16 Aug
Adrian Spillett percussion 29 Aug
Dalia Stasevska conductor 30 Jul
John Storgårds conductor 10 Aug
Moses Sumney* singer 21 Aug

—T

Robin Ticciati conductor 31 Aug
Bramwell Tovey conductor 2 Sep
Thomas Trotter organ 4 Sep

—V

Miina-Liisa Värelä* soprano 31 Aug
Ilan Volkov conductor 26 Aug

—W

Adam Walker flute P@CH 4, 29 Aug
Omer Meir Wellber conductor 3 Aug
Nardus Williams* soprano 16 Aug
Roderick Williams baritone 9 Sep
John Wilson conductor 4 Sep

GROUPS

Academy of St Martin in the Fields 25 Aug
Arcangelo 9 Sep
Arcangelo Chorus 9 Sep
Aurora Orchestra 11 Aug
BBC Concert Orchestra 31 Jul, 2, 6 Sep
BBC National Orchestra of Wales 2, 8, 15 Aug
BBC Philharmonic 3, 10, 16 Aug
BBC Scottish Symphony Orchestra 6, 26, 28 Aug
BBC Singers 30 Jul, 19 Aug, 11 Sep
BBC Symphony Orchestra 30 Jul, 13, 21, 27 Aug, 3, 11 Sep
Bournemouth Symphony Orchestra 9 Aug
Chesaba* 15 Aug
Chineke! Orchestra 24 Aug
City of Birmingham Symphony Orchestra 5 Aug
English Baroque Soloists 1 Sep
Glyndebourne Festival Opera 31 Aug
Hallé 7 Sep
London Philharmonic Orchestra 12, 31 Aug
London Symphony Orchestra 22 Aug
Mahler Chamber Orchestra 30 Aug
Manchester Collective* 17 Aug
Marian Consort* P@CH 2
Marmen Quartet* P@CH 3
Monteverdi Choir 1 Sep
National Youth Orchestra of Great Britain 7 Aug
Philharmonia Orchestra 14 Aug
Royal Liverpool Philharmonic Orchestra 5 Sep
Royal Philharmonic Orchestra 4 Aug
Scottish Chamber Orchestra 1 Aug
Sinfonia of London* 4 Sep

Index of Works

P@CH indicates 'Proms at ... Cadogan Hall' chamber music concerts

*first performance at a BBC Henry Wood Promenade Concert

A

Thomas Adès (born 1971)
The Exterminating Angel Symphony*
London premiere **5 Aug**
Thomas Arne (1710–78)
Rule, Britannia! (arr. Sargent) **11 Sep**
Malcolm Arnold (1921–2006)
Symphony No. 5* **27 Aug**

B

Johann Sebastian Bach (1685–1750)
Christ lag in Todes Banden, BWV 4 **1 Sep**
14 Canons, BWV 1087 (Goldberg Variations)
(orch. Goldmann)* **12 Aug**
Keyboard Concerto in F minor,
BWV 1056 **14 Aug**
St Matthew Passion **9 Sep**
Béla Bartók (1881–1945)
Violin Concerto No. 2 **28 Aug**
Mason Bates (born 1977)
Auditorium* UK premiere **9 Aug**
Ludwig van Beethoven (1770–1827)
Concert aria 'Ah! perfido' **26 Aug**
Piano Concerto No. 4 in G major **7 Sep**
Symphony No. 2 in D major **26 Aug**
Symphony No. 3 in E flat major, Eroica' **7 Aug**
Symphony No. 4 in B flat major **3 Aug**
George Benjamin (born 1960)
Concerto for Orchestra* BBC co-commission:
world premiere **30 Aug**
Alban Berg (1885–1935)
Seven Early Songs **4 Sep**
Eugène Bozza (1905–91)
Fantaisie pastorale* **P@CH 5**

Johannes Brahms (1833–97)
Clarinet Trio in A minor, Op. 114* **P@CH 1**
Symphony No. 4 in E minor **2 Aug**
Charlotte Bray (born 1982)
Where Icebergs Dance Away*
UK premiere **27 Aug**
William Byrd (c1540–1623)
Ave verum corpus **19 Aug**
Britta Byström (born 1977)
Parallel Universes* BBC commission:
world premiere **10 Aug**

C

Sethus Calvisius (1556–1615)
Praeter rerum seriem* **P@CH 2**
Unsuk Chin (born 1961)
Subito con forza* BBC co-commission:
UK premiere **7 Sep**
Samuel Coleridge-Taylor (1875–1912)
Hiawatha's Wedding Feast – overture
24 Aug
Symphony in A minor* **24 Aug**

D

Henri Dutilleux (1916–2013)
Oboe Sonata* **P@CH 5**
Antonín Dvořák (1841–1904)
Cello Concerto in B minor **5 Sep**
Symphony No. 9 in E minor, 'From the New
World' **8 Aug**

E

Julius Eastman (1940–90)
The Holy Presence of Joan d'Arc* **17 Aug**

Edward Elgar (1857–1934)
Cello Concerto in E minor **9 Aug**
Pomp and Circumstance March No. 1 in
D major ('Land of Hope and Glory') **11 Sep**

F

Shiva Feshareki (born 1987)
Aether World* BBC commission:
world premiere **19 Aug**
Edmund Finnis (born 1984)
The Centre is Everywhere* **17 Aug**

G

Ruth Gipps (1921–99)
Sea-Shore Suite* **P@CH 5**
Symphony No. 2 in B major* **5 Aug**
Phillip Glass (born 1937)
Mad Rush **6 Sep**
Henryk Górecki (1933–2010)
Harpsichord Concerto* **17 Aug**

H

George Frideric Handel (1685–1759)
Dixit Dominus **1 Sep**
Donna, che in ciel* **1 Sep**
Joseph Haydn (1732–1809)
String Quartet in D major, Op. 64 No. 5
'Lark'* **P@CH 3**
Paul Hindemith (1895–1963)
Symphony 'Mathis der Maler' **12 Aug**
Symphonic Metamorphosis of Themes by
Carl Maria von Weber **5 Sep**
Joseph Horovitz (born 1926)
Jazz Concerto* **17 Aug**

I

Charles Ives (1874–1954)
Three Places in New England
(Orchestral Set No. 1) **8 Aug**

J

Leoš Janáček (1854–1928)
Taras Bulba **9 Aug**
Josquin des Prez (c1450/55–1521)
Benedicta es, caelorum regina **P@CH 2**

**Index of
Works**

Inviolata, integra et casta es *P@CH 2*
Praeter rerum seriem* *P@CH 2*
Qui habitat in adiutorio altissimi (a 24)
19 Aug
Laura Jurd *(born 1990)*
new work* *London premiere* **7 Aug**

— K

Oliver Knussen *(1952–2018)*
The Way to Castle Yonder **30 Aug**
Erich Wolfgang Korngold *(1897–1957)*
Symphony in F sharp major **4 Sep**

— L

George Lewis *(born 1952)*
Minds in Flux* *BBC commission:*
world premiere **26 Aug**
Franz Liszt *(1818–86)* Fantasy and Fugue
on 'Ad nos, ad salutarem undam' **4 Sep**
Vicente Lusitano *(died after 1561)*
Inviolata, integra et casta es* *P@CH 2*

— M

Sir James MacMillan *(born 1959)*
new work* *BBC co-commission: world
premiere* **30 Jul**
Grace-Evangeline Mason *(born 1994)*
The Imagined Forest* *BBC co-commission:
world premiere* **5 Sep**
Felix Mendelssohn *(1809–47)*
Symphony No. 5 in D major,
'Reformation' **4 Aug**
Ella Milch-Sheriff *(born 1954)*
The Eternal Stranger* *BBC co-commission:
UK premiere* **3 Aug**
Samy Moussa *(born 1984)*
A Globe Itself Infolding* **6 Sep**
Wolfgang Amadeus Mozart *(1756–91)*
Piano Concerto No. 24 in C minor,
K491 **14 Aug**
Symphony No. 39 in E flat major **1 Aug**
Symphony No. 40 in G minor **1 Aug**
Symphony No. 41 in C major, 'Jupiter' **1 Aug**
Nico Muhly *(born 1981)*
A New Flame (after Sweelinck)*
BBC commission: world premiere **19 Aug**

— O

Elizabeth Ogonek *(born 1989)*
Cloudine* *BBC co-commission:
world premiere* **2 Aug**

— P

Hubert Parry *(1848–1918)*
Jerusalem (orch. Elgar) **11 Sep**
Giovanni Battista Pergolesi *(1710–36)*
Stabat mater **6 Aug**
Astor Piazzolla *(1921–92)*
The Four Seasons of Buenos Aires
(arr. Desyatnikov) **25 Aug**
Francis Poulenc *(1899–1963)*
Oboe Sonata* *P@CH 4*
Organ Concerto **30 Jul**
Florence Price *(1887–1953)*
Piano Concerto in One Movement* **24 Aug**
Sergey Prokofiev *(1891–1953)*
Symphony No. 1 in D major, 'Classical'
14 Aug
Henry Purcell *(1659–95)*
Dido and Aeneas – 'When I am laid in earth'
(Dido's Lament) (arr. Stokowski) **2 Aug**
Fantasias (orch. George Benjamin)*
world premiere **30 Aug**

— R

Sergey Rachmaninov *(1873–1943)*
Rhapsody on a Theme of Paganini **11 Aug**
Ariel Ramírez *(1921–2010)*
songs* *P@CH 4*
Maurice Ravel *(1875–1937)*
Piano Concerto in G major **30 Aug**
La valse **4 Sep**
Ottorino Respighi *(1879–1936)*
Concerto gregoriano* **4 Aug**

— S

Camille Saint-Saëns *(1835–1921)*
The Carnival of the Animals **29 Aug**
Cello Concerto No. 1 in A minor **2 Aug**
Fantaisie in E flat major **4 Sep**
Oboe Sonata* *P@CH 5*
Symphony No. 3 in C minor, 'Organ' **7 Sep**

Franz Schubert *(1797–1828)*
Symphony No. 2 in B flat major **3 Aug**
Dmitry Shostakovich *(1906–75)*
Symphony No. 9 in E flat major **14 Aug**
Robert Simpson *(1921–97)*
String Quartet No. 1* *P@CH 3*
Fela Sowande *(1905–87)*
African Suite* **24 Aug**
Johann Strauss II *(1825–99)*
Die Fledermaus – overture **4 Sep**
Richard Strauss *(1864–1949)*
Don Juan **5 Sep**
Igor Stravinsky *(1882–1971)*
The Firebird – suite (1945) **11 Aug**
Jeu de cartes **12 Aug**
Otche nash **19 Aug**
Pulcinella **6 Aug**
Symphonies of Wind Instruments **22 Aug**
Symphony in C **22 Aug**
Symphony in Three Movements **22 Aug**
Jan Pieterszoon Sweelinck *(1562–1621)*
Je sens en moy une flamme
nouvelle* **19 Aug**

— T

Dobrinka Tabakova *(born 1980)*
Suite in Old Style, 'The Court Jester
Amareu'* **17 Aug**
Auga Read Thomas *(born 1964)*
Dance Foldings* *BBC commission:
world premiere* **8 Aug**
Traditional
Auld Lang Syne **11 Sep**
The National Anthem (arr. Britten) **11 Sep**

— V

Ralph Vaughan Williams *(1872–1958)*
Fantasia on a Theme by Thomas Tallis
4 Aug
Antonio Vivaldi *(1678–1741)*
The Four Seasons **25 Aug**

BBC Proms 2021

Director, BBC Proms David Pickard
Controller, BBC Radio 3 Alan Davey
Personal Assistant Yvette Pusey

Editor, BBC Radio 3 Emma Bloxham

Head of Marketing, Learning and Publications Kate Finch

Business Sanoma Evans (Business Advisor), Tricia Twigg (Co-ordinator)

Concerts and Planning Helen Heslop (Manager), Hannah Donat (Artistic Producer), Alys Jones, Helen White (Event Producers), Victoria Gunn (Event Co-ordinator)

Marketing Emily Caket (Manager), Sanjeet Riat (Executive)

Press and Communications Camilla Dervan (Communications Manager), Samantha Johnston (Publicist), Helena Bartholomew (Assistant Publicist)

Learning Lauren Creed, Ellara Wakely (Senior Learning Managers), Siân Bateman, Alison Dancer, Chloe Shrimpton (Learning Managers), Catherine Humphrey, Molly Wickham (Learning Co-ordinators)

Music Television Jan Younghusband (Head of Commissioning, BBC Music TV), Livewire Pictures Ltd (Production)

Digital Rory Connolly (Commissioning Executive, BBC Pop), Rhian Roberts (Head of Content Commissioning, Speech and Classical Music), David Prudames (Assistant Commissioner, BBC Music Digital)

BBC Music Library Tim Auvache, Anne Butcher, Natalie Dewar, Raymond Howden, Alison John, Michael Jones, Richard Malton, Claire Martin, Steven Nunes, David Russell, Joseph Schultz, Chris Williams

Commercial Rights & Business Affairs Katie Baum, Simon Brown, Sue Dickson, Hilary Dodds, Dan Partridge, Ashley Smith, Pamela Wise

BBC Proms Publications

Publishing Manager Christine Webb
Editorial Manager Edward Bhesania
Sub-Editor Timmy Fisher
Publications Designer Reenie Basova
Publications Co-ordinator Deborah Fether

Advertising Cabbells (020 3603 7930); cabbells.co.uk
Cover illustration BBC Creative/BBC
Published by BBC Proms Publications, Room 3015, Broadcasting House, London W1A 1AA
Distributed by Bloomsbury Publishing, 50 Bedford Square, London WC1B 3DP

Printed by APS Group

APS Group holds ISO 14001 environmental management, FSC® and PEFC certifications. Printed using vegetable-based inks on FSC-certified paper. Formed in 1993 as a response to concerns over global deforestation, FSC (Forest Stewardship Council®) is an independent, non-governmental, not-for-profit organisation established to promote the responsible management of the world's forests. For more information, please visit www.fsc-uk.org.

In line with the BBC's sustainability strategy, the BBC Proms is actively working with partners and suppliers towards being a more sustainable festival.

ISBN 978-1-912114-08-5

— W

Richard Wagner *(1813–83)*
Tristan and Isolde **31 Aug**

William Walton *(1902–83)*
Cello Concerto **12 Aug**
Viola Concerto **27 Aug**

Adrian Willaert *(c1490–1562)*
Benedicta es, caelorum regina* **P@CH 2**

Roderick Williams *(born 1965)*
Ave Verum Corpus Re-imagined* **19 Aug**

arr. Wood *(1869–1944)*
Fantasia on British Sea-Songs **11 Sep**

— Z

Alexander von Zemlinsky *(1871–1942)*
Clarinet Trio in D minor, Op. 3* **P@CH 1**

MISCELLANEOUS

20th-Century British Film Music **2 Sep**
Bartók Roots **28 Aug**
Family Prom **29 Aug**
First Night of the Proms 2021 **30 Jul**
The Golden Age of Broadway **31 Jul**
Last Night of the Proms 2021 **11 Sep**
Moses Sumney Meets Jules Buckley and the BBC Symphony Orchestra **21 Aug**
Organ Recital **1 Aug, 4 Sep**
Pauline Viardot and Her Circle **P@CH 6**
To Soothe the Aching Heart (opera excerpts) **16 Aug**

Index of Works